Numbers

Faith in the Wilderness

If the L*ORD* *delights in us, He will bring us into this land and give it to us, a land that flows with milk and honey.*

Numbers 14:8

Timothy A. Rake

CONCORDIA PUBLISHING HOUSE · SAINT LOUIS

3558 S. Jefferson Avenue

St. Louis, MO 63118–3968

1-800-325-3040 • www.cph.org

Written by Timothy A. Rake

Edited by Robert C. Baker

This publication may be available in braille, in large print, or on cassette tape for the visually impaired. Please allow 8 to 12 weeks for delivery. Write to Lutheran Blind Mission, 7550 Watson Rd., St. Louis, MO 63119-4409; call toll-free 1-888-215-2455; or visit the Web site: www.blindmission.org.

1 2 3 4 5 6 7 8 9 10 16 15 14 13 12 11 10 09 08 07

Contents

History	*Date (BC)*	*Numbers*
Joseph born *(Genesis 30:22–24)*	ca. **1915**	
Jacob settles in Egypt *(Genesis 46:5–7)*	**1876**	
Hammurabi begins reign in Babylonia	**1792**	
	1526	Moses born in Egypt *(Exodus 2:1–8)*
Amenhotep II becomes Pharaoh of Egypt	**1450**	
Exodus from Egypt	**1446**	*(Exodus 12:31–51)*
Hebrews wander in the wilderness	**1446–1406**	Moses writes Pentateuch *(Genesis–Deuteronomy)*
Construction of Tabernacle *(Exodus 25–30; 35–40)*	**1446**	
	1444	Moses and Aaron take census *(Numbers 1:1–46)*; send spies to Canaan *(Numbers 13:1–3; 28)*
Aaron dies on Mt. Hor *(Numbers 33:38–39)*	**1406**	Moses dies on Mt. Nebo *(Deuteronomy 34)*
Joshua leads Hebrews into Canaan; Conquest begins *(Joshua 1–3)*	**1405**	
Joshua dies *(Joshua 24:29)*	**1399**	

An Outline of Numbers

The Book of Numbers can be divided into three main sections, mostly based upon the geographical setting. Section 1 occurs near Sinai (1:1–10:10); section 2, near Kadesh (10:11–22:1); and section 3 occurs in the plains of Moab (22:2–36:13). The book also can be arranged according to the major events of the narrative, which might look as follows: part 1, Israel's obedience (chs. 1–10); part 2, Israel's disobedience (chs. 11–25); and part 3, (new) Israel's obedience (chs. 26–36).

I. Israel at Sinai, Preparing for the Promised Land (1:1–10:10)
- A. The Commands for Census of the People (chs. 1–4)
  - 1. The Men Numbered for War (1:1–54)
  - 2. The Arrangement of the Tribes (chs. 2–3)
  - 3. The Levitical Service (ch. 4)
- B. The People Prepared and Purified (5:1–10:10)
  - 1. Purity in the Camp (chs. 5–6)
  - 2. The Priesthood and the Temple Services (7–9:14)
  - 3. God Meets with His People (9:15–10:10)

II. The Journey from Sinai to Kadesh (1:11–12:16)
- A. The Beginning of the Journey (10:1–11:36)
- B. The Beginning of Sorrows: Fire and Quail (ch. 11)
- C. The Opposition of Miriam and Aaron (ch. 12)

III. Israel at Kadesh (13:1–20:13)
- A. The Twelve Spies (ch. 13)
- B. The People's Rebellion (ch. 14)
- C. Various Laws (ch. 15)
- D. The Insurrection of Korah (ch. 16)
- E. The Test of Aaron's Rod (ch. 17)
- F. Levitical Duties (ch. 18)
- G. The Red Heifer (ch. 19)
- H. Moses' Great Sin (20:1–13)

IV. The Journey From Kadesh to Moab (20:14–2:1)
- A. The Resistance of Edom (20:14–21)
- B. The Death of Aaron (20:22–29)
- C. The Destruction of Arad (21:1–3)
- D. The Bronze Serpent (21:4–9)

- E. Conflict and Victory (21:10–22:1)

V. Israel Prepares to Enter the Land (22:2–32:42)

- A. Balaam, Balak, and Baal (chs. 22–25)
- B. The Second Census (ch. 26)
- C. Instructions for the New Generation (chs. 27–30)
- D. War Against Midian (ch. 31)
- E. The inheritance of Reuben, Gad, and half of Manasseh (ch. 32)

VI. Final Matters (chs. 33–36)

- A. The Journey Recalled (ch. 33)
- B. The Land and Laws of Inheritance (chs. 34–36)

Introduction

The Book of Numbers is the divine record of Israel's experience from the time of the Exodus until their entrance into the Promised Land forty years later. God prepared His people to take possession of the Promised Land by bringing them into conformity with His Law. Numbers' primary theme is the testing of faith, showing how God by His grace leads His people through wilderness wanderings to their promised destination. God does this despite the disobedience of His people. Woven throughout the book is the promise of salvation by grace alone, along with the warning that unbelief, as the rejection of that grace, leads only to spiritual disaster and the loss of God's gifts. God calls His people to believe His gracious promise and to rely upon Him solely by faith. He assures them that by His power He alone will sustain their lives and subdue their enemies. Through the ordeals of testing and trial, God nurtures and strengthens their faith so that they come to know the reality and truthfulness of God's Word.

The types and shadows of Christ that fill the Old Testament are found throughout Numbers. Israel's failure under the Law demonstrates that, apart from God's acting on our behalf, it is impossible for His will to be done in our lives. We must die and be made new again, as Israel learned corporately.

The New Testament cites or alludes to Numbers several times. For example, the rock from which water was made to flow in Numbers 20 is mentioned in 1 Corinthians 10:4 and is said to have been Christ. Perhaps most well known is John 3:14, where Jesus notes that the Son of Man must be raised on the cross as "Moses lifted up the serpent in the wilderness" (Numbers 21:6–9). We should also mention the infamous false prophet Balaam (Numbers 22–25), whom the New Testament holds forth as one who conducts ministry for earthly gain (2 Peter 2:15–16; Jude 11; Revelation 2:14).

In the Book of Numbers, as in all of Scripture, we find the story of God's redemption of sinners by His grace alone.

Lesson 1

The First Census of God's People

Chapters 1 through 4 of Numbers contain the first official census, or detailed counting, recorded about the camp of Israel. (A previous census to assess an atonement tax is mentioned in Exodus 38:25–26.) Included, as well, are specifications for the arrangement of the tribes around the Tent of Meeting (the tabernacle) and their formation when encamped or when marching. All of this is in preparation for Israel to enter and take possession of the land of Canaan.

Counting the People

Chapter 1 records the first census which takes place at Mount Sinai. This occurs a year and two months after the Israelites left Egypt during the Exodus. God's people are preparing for war in the land of promise, where they will, by God's power, drive out "seven nations more numerous and mightier" than they (Deuteronomy 7:1). Here, God commands that every tribe and family be counted and that from them males twenty years of age and older—"all in Israel who are able to go to war"—are to be numbered individually. God then commands that certain named persons from each tribe will assist Moses and Aaron in making the census (vv. 5–16). These men are tribal leaders and are mentioned elsewhere in Numbers (2:1–24; 7:1–88; 10:14–28).

However, the census is not initiated by Moses' personal interest or some strategic military plan that he had conceived. Rather, in verse 1 of chapter 1, we are told that "the LORD spoke to Moses" and ordered the census. God did not order the census for His own benefit, to prove to Himself or even to His people how "successful" He was, or to vindicate Himself. He did not command the census to be taken to make His people feel secure in knowing their size. The divine purpose of this census was, first, for God to acknowledge His people graciously as His own and, second, for Him to make and mark their place in the Holy Congregation.

1. Read Numbers 1:1–46; 2 Samuel 24:1–17; and 1 Chronicles 21:1–17. How does David's numbering of the people differ from that of Moses' in Numbers?

The census required that males, twenty years old and older, be counted as they are "able to go to war" (Numbers 1:3). Note how elsewhere in this chapter that expression recurs (vv. 20, 22, 24, 26, 28, 30, 32, 34, 36, 38, 40, 42, and 45). Just as these men are naturally mature, God desires and expects us to become spiritually mature (Ephesians 4:15; 1 Peter 2:2; 2 Peter 3:18). Spiritual maturity brings with it an experiential knowledge and acquaintance with God's grace that enable us to overcome the devil through faith alone (see 1 John 2:13–14).

2. How does this section from Numbers apply to us as Christians, especially as Jesus Christ has fought and won for us the great battle of salvation (see Luke 11:22; John 16:33; 1 John 4:4; Revelation 12:11)?

In verses 20–44, the tallies of each tribe are given. The sum total is 603,550 men who are twenty years old and older (v. 46). This is exactly the number given of a previous counting (not a military census as in Numbers) of men twenty and older (Exodus 38:26). Critical scholars point to this as evidence that the Pentateuch (the first five books of the Bible whose human authorship was ascribed by Jesus Himself to Moses; see Mark 12:26; Luke 16:29, 31) has been edited and reworked by subsequent scribes in order to appear uniform. However, this conclusion is both unnecessary and speculative. Later in Numbers, at the second great census, the total differs: 601,730 (Numbers 26:51). If a later editor had intended to make these figures artificially match, then he would have naturally been inclined to do so elsewhere; but he doesn't. The inclusion of these figures, which represent human beings, serves to remind us of God's grace and that He knows "those who are His" (2 Timothy 2:19) and that none will be lost (John 17:12).

3. Why does faith not stumble at this remarkable coincidence, rather regarding God's Word as true despite what reason and our senses may tell us?

4. Read Revelation 7:1–8 and 14:1–5. How does God "count" His elect people? Why are attempts to judge our faithfulness to God based upon human and visible numbering misleading?

Read 1:47–54. Excluded from the census is the tribe of Levi, or the Levites (v. 47). The Levites were not eligible for military duty, but were devoted exclusively to the service of the tabernacle. Thcy were appointed to care for, tend the services of, and see to the transport of the tabernacle. In addition, the Levites were directed to pitch their tents in closest permissible proximity to the Tent of Meeting on all sides in order to surround it with their presence. This reminded non-Levites that, according to the Law, only by the ministry of the Levitical priesthood could access be granted to God. Not everyone was called to public ministry, though all were members of the Holy Nation.

5. Read Luke 16:13, Titus 1:5, and Hebrews 13:17. Explain how, although all Christians are servants, all are not ministers.

6. The Book of Hebrews (see 7:22; 8:6; 9:33) in the New Testament teaches that a "better" priesthood in Jesus Christ has replaced the Levitical priesthood. How does Jesus fulfill the duties mentioned in 1:50–51 and keep God's "wrath" (v. 53), once and for all, from falling upon us?

Arrangements for the Camp

God commanded the orderly arrangement of the twelve tribes around both the tabernacle and the Levites. (The tribe of Joseph was divided according to his sons, Manasseh and Ephraim, with the Levites left uncounted.) This arrangement reflected the necessity of God's people to be in conformity with the divine will. Human beings, by themselves, cannot bring their lives into alignment with God's righteous standards. Although there was doubtlessly some practical military wisdom in the tribal formation, its value and meaning were not found in human strength or prowess. Rather, the arrangement meant that God was at the center of their corporate lives, and every tent (life) was facing Him (2:2). The tribes were assigned their place when encamped. Groups of three were on each side (2:1–34). When marching, six were in front, and six were in back.

7. Just as God had a place for each member of this body of people, so He has in Christ a place for each Christian in Christ's body, the Church (see 1 Corinthians 12 and 14). What insight does Numbers 2 provide for understanding how we relate to our respective congregations and carry out God's will?

8. The tribes were situated on all four sides of the tabernacle. Yet, there was only one entrance. This entrance was accessible only by Moses and the house of Aaron, who were encamped in front of the tabernacle (3:38). Consider the city of God envisioned in Revelation 21:1–13. There is no need of a temple there, since God and His people dwell together as one. Open gates stand on all four sides. What is the significance of this, and how might it relate to the camp arrangements of Numbers 2?

Three entities are responsible for leading God's people: Judah, Moses, and the Levites. *Judah* is the lead tribe that follows the directions given by the Lord through *Moses* (9:23), with a small band of *Levites* marching before them bearing the ark of the covenant (10:17–21).

9. How does Christ fulfill all three of these roles? How are Christians kept aligned with God's righteousness by following Him (see Luke 9:62; Romans 8:1; 2 Corinthians 2:13; Galatians 5:25; 6:16)?

Counting the Levites

Chapters 3 and 4 record a separate census being taken of the tribe of Levi. The census has two parts. The first counts all males older than one month of age (3:14); the second count all males between the ages of thirty and fifty who are able-bodied (4:2).

From the tribe of Levi, the family of Aaron, Moses' brother, is set apart. Only priests from this family may touch the altar, offer sacrifices, or approach the tabernacle (3:1–4). Their duty was so serious that failure to comply strictly with the divinely prescribed laws of worship resulted in judgment from God. Verse 4 alludes to the death of two of Aaron's sons, Nadab and Abihu (Leviticus 10:1–2), who were struck down by God for offering "unauthorized [strange] fire."

10. Why do you think that the Book of Leviticus mentions this event? Is it a word of Gospel or Law?

In chapter 4, the Kohathites (the family of Kohath of the tribe of Levi) were charged with the transport of the tabernacle and all its furnishings. Yet, only the Aaronites (descendants of Aaron) were allowed to set it up and take it down. The Kohathites were warned that if they touched (4:15) or looked at (4:20) the "holy things" (uncovered) they would die at God's hand.

11. The New Testament applies the description "kingdom of priests" (Exodus 19:6) to the entire Church (1 Peter 2:9; Revelation 5:10; 20:6). How does the life of an individual perform priestly service unto God?

In Closing

Encourage participants to begin the following activities:

- Read Exodus 25–30, 35–39, and Leviticus 8–10, and familiarize yourself with the priesthood and the tabernacle.
- Read Hebrews 5–10 and consider how Christ fulfills the entire Levitical system in His person and work.
- Read Numbers 5:1–10:10 to prepare for the next session.

Close with prayer.

Lesson 2

God's Demands for Purity

This section, Numbers 5:1–10:10, continues with Israel's preparation to enter the Promised Land. They remain situated at Mount Sinai after having received the Law and its detailed instruction for being God's holy people. Chapters 5 and 6 stress the necessity of purity within the camp. In 7:1–9:14, matters related to the priesthood and the service of the tabernacle are taken up.

This section of Numbers concludes with the narrative of God's presence in the form of a fiery cloud above the tabernacle. It also gives instructions for God's people to be called to assembly on various occasions through two special silver trumpets (9:15–10:10).

The Camp Cleansed

God chose to dwell in the camp of Israel (5:3). Consequently, the camp was to be holy. According to the Law, this called for purity and the removal of things and persons that were defiled. Anyone who was "leprous [a general term for various skin diseases] or has a discharge and everyone who is unclean through contact with the dead" had to be expelled (5:2). Although Leviticus 12–15 describes conditions for how one may be pronounced clean, there was no promise that such a pronouncement would be made. Until such time, those who had been expelled were required to live apart from the rest of the people (see Leviticus 13:45–46, which tells of "lepers" who were required to live in disgrace).

12. Although harsh and alienating, these prescriptions of the Law made the camp clean. Contrast how Christ makes people clean not by separating Himself from such people, but by touching them and joining them to Himself (see Matthew 8:2–4; Mark 1:40–45).

Following a brief instruction regarding restitution (5:5–10), there is an extended account of the case of a woman suspected of adultery. A rather elaborate ritual is prescribed for a priestly testing of a man's wife when he believes her to be guilty of infidelity. Here, we note two things: first, she is to be set "before the LORD," and, second, the grain offering is not for atonement but for "bringing iniquity to remembrance" (v. 15). This means that the verdict is delivered by the Lord and not the husband, and that the Law's purpose here is to expose sin and remedy it through penal judgment if sin is discovered.

13. Read Luke 7:36–50 and John 8:2–11. How does Christ bring about justice for adulterous people in contrast to the Law? Does He expose or remove sin?

The Nazirites formed a unique and voluntary religious order within Israelite society. Though not priests, their form of life was similar in its singular devotion to God (6:2). Men or women could commit themselves to God for a period of time through a "special vow" that required them to abstain from all grape products or alcohol, to leave their hair uncut, and to avoid coming near or contacting a dead body (vv. 3–8).

The Nazirite reminded God's people that their lives belong to Him and that purity of life is found only in relationship to God. The peculiar way the Law shows devotion to God really portrays the spiritual character of Christ and God's people found only in Christ.

14. Read Matthew 2:23 and Romans 12:1–2. In what sense is Christ the fulfillment of the Nazirite order, and what does it mean for our lives in relation to God?

15. Chapter 6 ends with the famous Aaronic blessing (vv. 24–26). What might be the purpose of placing this benediction at the end of a

section on purity regulations, and how does this "put [the LORD'S] name upon the people of Israel" (v. 27)?

Worshiping the Lord

In this section, 7:1–9:14, the text centers on the service of the tabernacle. Chapter 7, the longest in all the Pentateuch, concerns offerings brought by the heads or "chiefs" of each tribe. The gifts brought from Judah to Naphtali are described in detail. Chronologically, this precedes chapters 1 through 6 by one month.

Some scholars suggest that this arrangement of materials serves to connect the prosperity of God's people, seen in the richness of their gifts, with the priesthood. God's people are able to bring freely and generously their gifts to the altar because God has pronounced His blessing over them.

16. What sacrifices do Christians, as royal priests, offer in view of Christ (see Ephesians 5:2; Philippians 4:18; Hebrews 13:15–16; 1 Peter 2:5)?

Worship and service required purity before God. Chapter 8 describes the purification ritual laid out before the Levites. This rite is similar to that performed for the priests (Exodus 29; Leviticus 8–9). The instructions are given twice, with the second set in reverse order. God took elaborate steps to provide suitable servants for His people.

17. How should we treat those whom God sets apart for public ministry? How should we regard them (see Luke 10:16 and 11:49)?

Once more, the time had come to observe the Passover. This feast, as one of five feasts of Israel (see Leviticus 23; Numbers 28–29), celebrates the miraculous deliverance of Israel from slavery in Egypt. The Passover was to be kept "according to all its statutes and all its rules" (9:3), which meant that the festival must begin on the fourteenth day of the first month. It was to last for eight days.

The only exceptions to this Passover regulation was either for someone whose journey was prohibited by distance or for someone who had become ritually unclean through contact with a dead body (v. 10). Deliberate contempt for the Passover resulted in excommunication from the people (v. 13).

18. Christ is our true Passover (1 Corinthians 5:7). What may be said of those who deliberately neglect or have contempt for the Lord's Supper?

God Himself Is Present

This final section (9:15–10:10) focuses on two events as Israel sets to begin its journey to Kadesh. One was God's presence in the form of a cloud that stood over the tabernacle. At night, the cloud had "the appearance of fire" (9:15). The other event was the appointment of a set of special silver trumpets to summon God's people and to remind them of their covenant relationship He made with them (10:10).

Exodus 40:34–38 mentioned the presence of this cloud in connection with the tabernacle, which is seen even earlier in the Exodus (Exodus 13:21–22). God's presence is revealed only when this sacred Tent of Meeting is erected.

19. On the Mount of Transfiguration (see Matthew 17:1–8; Mark 9:2–8; Luke 9:28–36), we see Christ as the true tabernacle. What does this mean for our lives and the Church's ministry?

To signal to His people that the time for marching had come, God lifted the cloud of His presence off the tabernacle. He graciously added another means to announce this (and other occasions for assembly) to His people. Not only did He provide a visible sign, He also provided an audible one, as well. These were joined together to summon God's people to march by faith through the wilderness.

20. How has God done the same for us as Christians (see Hebrews 12:19 and Revelation 1:10)?

In Closing

Encourage participants to begin the following activities:

- Read Leviticus 11–15 and review how important ritual and social purity were in God's Law.
- Review the first Passover and its institution in Exodus 12–14 and Leviticus 23:4–8.
- Discuss the difference between holiness by the Law and holiness by the Gospel.
- Read Numbers 10:11–12:16 to prepare for the next session.

Close with prayer.

Lesson 3

The Journey from Sinai to Kadesh

The next major section in Numbers stretches from 10:11 to 20:13, which takes up the journey from Sinai to Kadesh and Israel's long stay at Kadesh. A total of thirty-eight years transpires during this time.

In this section, we see how God tests the faith of His people through one trial after another. Later, Moses will explain that this ordeal was from God. God intended through their trials that His people might come to know and believe that He—the Lord alone—is God, that He alone saves and delivers, and that they must know in their sinful hearts there is no good (Deuteronomy 8:1–6).

The readers of Numbers will find a familiarity in the trials and events taking place during the Israelite's time of testing. Both Exodus and Numbers display a "pattern" of redemption. The same lesson of human sinfulness (our guilt and God's holy wrath against it) and divine grace must be learned over and over again: Exodus 15:22–26 and Numbers 11:1–3 (murmuring of the people); Exodus 16 and Numbers 11:4–13 and 31–35 (manna from heaven and quail); Exodus 17:1–7 and Numbers 20:1–13 (water from the rock); Exodus 18 and Numbers 10:29–11:30 (advice from in-laws and leaders chosen); Exodus 17:8–16 and Numbers 14:39–45 (the Amalekites defeated).

The first part of this period, on which lesson 3 of our booklet focuses, is the journey to Kadesh (10:11–12:16). The narrative is built chiefly around three events: first, the commencement of the journey (10:11–36); second, the first set of trials (11); third, opposition to Moses (12).

21. How does God use trials to strengthen our faith? What is our natural reaction when God permits difficulties, aggravations, peril, and tragedy to occur?

Beginning the Journey

God signaled to His people to begin their march by lifting the cloud of His presence. (In rabbinical literature, this came to be called the *shekinah*, meaning God's "tabernacled" presence.) God's people begin their march to the desert of Paran (10:11–13) at Kadesh on its northern border (13:26). This is a journey of more than 150 miles that will take several days, with stops along the way at Kibroth-hattaavah and Hazeroth (11:35).

The marching order given in 10:14–28 is exactly the same as that given previously in 2:1–34. Here, God adds further instructions concerning the Levitical tribes of the Gershonites, Merarites, and Kohathites (vv. 17–21).

22. Why do you think the marching order is repeated? What does this say about the Law?

23. Moses invoked God's name in special ways whenever the ark of the covenant "set" or when "it rested" (Numbers 10:35–36). Why is this so, and what is the significance of Moses' words?

The First Trials

After a trek of three days in the desert, Israel was led to a place of temporary rest. Apparently, they encounter the kinds of difficulties and problems that such a large group of people traveling in arid land is likely to encounter (11:1, "misfortunes"). They complained "in the hearing of the LORD," which meant, in effect, they accused God of unfaithfulness.

In response, God destroyed some on the outskirts of the camp by a judgment of fire. The place was subsequently named *Tebarah*, which means "burning" (v. 3).

24. Does this response by God seem excessive? Why is it, in fact, perfectly just?

Following this incident, the people are disturbed by the moaning cries of the "rabble" among them. A year-long diet of manna (see Exodus 16) had "dried up" their strength (11:6). Who was this group of people, exactly? The Hebrew word for rabble (*asaphsuph*) denotes a loosely connected group of people thrown together. It likely refers to the non-Israelite hangers-on (such as slaves or the destitute) who joined with them in the Exodus.

The rabble infect the Israelites with their discontentment until Moses is overcome with distress. Moses asks God how he could possibly find food for all these people (11:13). They despise God's gifts and demand that the lusts of their flesh be satisfied instead (v. 4). In the end, God gives them what their sinful desire demands and, with it, the death that it brings (vv. 18–20 and 31–35).

25. What warnings does Scripture give to Christians regarding the influence of false brothers and unbelievers in their midst (see 1 Corinthians 5:6; Galatians 5:9; 2 Timothy 2:20–22)?

26. Read John 6:22–58. Who are the "rabble" there, and how do they despise Christ as the true manna? Why does Christ say that manna is not the "bread from heaven"?

Sensing his limits, Moses appealed to God for help to perform his tasks. God responded by appointing seventy elders to be special leaders alongside Moses and under his direction. These men were given a portion of the Spirit that was on Moses in order to equip them for their tasks (v. 17).

27. What is the connection between God's appointment of these leaders and the complaining by the people?

28. Read Luke 10:1–17. How does this parallel Numbers 11:16–

17 and 24–30? How does the Gospel reveal that under Christ this is fulfilled?

Divine Leadership Challenged

Chapter 12 records the challenge by Miriam and Aaron (Moses' sister and brother; see Exodus 15:20 and 4:14), to Moses' divinely appointed leadership as God's minister. Miriam and Aaron protested Moses' role as the supreme prophet (v. 2). The basis for their case was the flimsy criticism that Moses had married a Cushite woman (either his first wife, Zipporah, or after her death a second wife). The suggestion is that Moses had not acted in a God-pleasing way; he had erred in knowing the will of God. Miriam speaks for both (v. 1, "spoke" is literally "she spoke"), specifying Miriam as the one who is vocal). She is, after all, called a prophetess (Exodus 15:20).

God acted to vindicate Moses in two ways: first, He pointed out that He spoke with Moses exclusively "mouth to mouth" (v. 8); second, He afflicts Miriam with leprosy as punishment for her sin (v. 10).

29. What excuses do we often give, whether openly or secretly in our hearts, for despising Christ's ministers (see Mark 6:3; John 6:41–44; Galatians 4:12–16)?

30. How does Moses' intercession show us Christ and both the triumph of grace over sin and the Gospel as the fulfillment of Law?

In Closing

Encourage participants to begin the following activities:

- Discuss personal spiritual experiences and ask students to tell how their faith has been affected through trials.
- Read the following passages from Scripture that mention meekness to derive a biblical definition of it: Psalm 22:26; 25:9; 147:6; 149:4; Isaiah 61:1; Matthew 5:5; 11:29; 21:5.
- Read Numbers 13:1–16:50 to prepare for the next session.

Close with prayer.

Lesson 4

Unbelief and Korah's Rebellion

At the end of chapter 12, we are told the people continue their wilderness march until they reach Kadesh (the wilderness of Paran). Tested by the Lord, here Israel repeatedly acts in willful unbelief, causing them to remain at Kadesh for an entire generation. Instead of entering the Promised Land (God knows well what kind of people they are; see Exodus 33:1–6), Israel is forced to wander in the desert for forty years (14:26–37).

This spans chapters 13 through 20, at the end of which time both Miriam (20:1) and Aaron die (20:22–29). With them passes an entire generation (those twenty and older at the beginning of the forty years of discipline; see 14:29).

In this session, we will look at three key events: first, the report and unbelief of the spies (13 and 14), except Caleb and Joshua; (see 13:30 and 14:30); second, additional laws of sacrifice (15:1–41); and third, the sedition led by a Levite (a Kohathite) named Korah (16:1–50).

31. What is the real nature of Israel's disobedience (see 14:11, 33)?

The Twelve Spies

Read chapters 13 and 14. God has led His people to Kadesh in the desert of Paran. This is the staging area for an invasion and conquest of Canaan, promised to them by the Lord (Exodus 3:17; 13:5).

Twelve spies, representing each of the tribes, are sent out on a forty-day scouting mission. Their orders are to bring back a report on the condition of things in the land. They return with proof of its agricultural abundance: a massive cluster of grapes along with figs and pomegranates (13:1–24).

However, ten of the spies testify that it is futile to attempt an invasion. The inhabitants of the land are described as being invincible, with cities built like fortresses, unusually (and perhaps unnaturally) large. This news is said to spread among the people as a "bad report" (v. 32).

God had promised to be with His people and to deliver the land to them (Exodus 23:31; Numbers 14:8–9). However, the people were poisoned with the unbelief of the ten spies and bitterly complained. In response, God threatened to destroy the entire camp and start anew. The people's sin is ripe for judgment. Only through Moses' intercession are the people spared. The temporal consequence of their sin is that they must wait forty years until the generation of the Exodus dies off.

32. Read Psalm 95 and Hebrews 3–4. Of what is Canaan a picture and promise? In what ways do we allow human reason and sense perception to undermine our faith? What is the true object of our faith?

33. How do Joshua and Caleb manifest a different spirit (see 13:30 and 14:6)? Why is their faith in the Gospel despised and even a threat to others (14:10)? Does this happen in the Christian Church?

Moses interceded once again for the people (14:13–19). Previously, he obtained God's mercy when they lapsed into idolatry at Sinai, worshiping a golden calf they had made (see Exodus 32).

34. What is the basis of Moses' plea for mercy from God? How is this, in fact, an invocation of the name of Christ (see Hebrews 11:26)?

Read Numbers 14:39–45. The people determined that they would enter the land despite being warned by Moses that they would not succeed. God was not with them. They piously disobeyed in the name of God's promise, only to discover they had acted again in unbelief.

35. How was their action a form of self-righteousness? Do we attempt to "make up" for our past sins in the same way? Why does this displease God?

More Laws of Sacrifice

Between chapters 14 and 16—in the middle of a narrative that focuses on Israel's disobedience—we find a brief word of instruction regarding sacrifice (15:1–37). To textual critics, this appears out of place, like the sloppy work of a later editor who mistakenly inserted cultic regulations meant for another context.

However, such cynicism is completely unwarranted. The change is not so abrupt as one might imagine. The failure of Israel's unbelief and God's judgment upon that generation make it all the more needful to hear a gracious word of promise. Will God not keep His Word and make provision for their sin?

Read Numbers 15. By beginning this section with the words "When you come into the land you are to inhabit" (15:2), God shines a light of hope that anticipates His fulfillment of the promise.

36. Read Romans 5:1–11 and 8:31–39. How does the sacrifice of Christ as our justification give us hope to endure life in a world under God's judgment?

This section falls naturally into three parts, all marked by the expression "the LORD spoke to Moses" (vv. 1, 17, 35). Through Moses, God reminds the Israelites of the righteousness of the Law: obedience to *all* the commandments of God (15:39–40). For sinners, the Law "brings wrath" (Romans 4:15) and spells death (Romans 7:9).

37. How does the case of the man stoned for gathering sticks on the Sabbath show the unrelenting severity of the Law? How is the Gospel different and how does it fulfill the Sabbath?

Korah's Rebellion

Read chapter 16. In this final portion of our lesson, we will look at the subversive attempt of Korah and his followers to overthrow God's rule through Moses (16:1–49). Korah was a Levite from the tribe of Kohath; therefore, he was in the service of the tabernacle. However, he had ambitions for the priesthood (16:10) and conspired with 250 other well-known leaders (see 16:2) to mutinously replace Moses and Aaron.

The Korah mob claimed that Moses had taken too much authority to himself (v. 13, "make yourself a prince") on the grounds that all of God's people were "holy" (v. 3). Moses turned to God once again for vindication as His servant (v. 5). God wished to "consume" the entire camp, but Moses' intercession spares most. So God destroyed Moses' enemies (who are, in fact, God's enemies, v. 11) by causing the earth to swallow them up and by sending a fire that consumed 250 of them (vv. 30–35).

Afterward, the people grumble and charge Moses with murder. God responded by sending a plague that killed 14,700 people (v. 49).

38. Read Jude 1:11. What class of people is compared to Korah? What is pastoral authority, and why do Christians sometimes think they may disregard it?

39. In what way does Moses intercede during the plague? How does verse 48 ("he stood between the dead and the living") speak of Christ?

In Closing

Encourage participants to begin the following activities:

- Read Exodus 20:8–11. Discuss the Old Testament law of the Sabbath.
- Discuss how opposition to the Gospel and ministers is handled in your congregation.
- Read Numbers 17:1–20:13 to prepare for the next session.

Close with prayer.

Lesson 5

Aaron and the Means of Grace

The final chapters of this section of Numbers (17:1–20:13) deal with the divine authority and power of the Aaronic priesthood and its duties, except for the closing portion of 20:1–13 (the account of Moses' great error). The temptation to neglect or even despise the priestly office was always close at hand. The ministry they performed was God's gift to His people and the means appointed by Him by which the gifts of salvation were to be dispensed. Therefore, any neglect or disregard of these gifts was disastrous. Here, we will learn how God wishes us to treasure the public ministry for its service of saving grace and by which means He makes known to people its divine glory.

God's Servant Vindicated

Read chapter 17. After judging Korah and his followers for their challenge to Moses and Aaron (and subsequently 14,700 of the people who later accused Moses and Aaron of murder), God instigates a trial on behalf of Aaron. Previously, it had been the people who were testing God, committing an audacious sin of unbelief (Exodus 17:2).

God has twelve staffs, one for each of the twelve tribes (with the tribal names being inscribed on the rods), collected and placed overnight in the tabernacle. The rod that blossomed by morning would indicate the one God had chosen as His servant (v. 5).

40. Is it ever right to "try" or "test" God (see Malachi 3:10)?

All of these staffs were pieces of dead wood. There was no earthly difference between these sticks, except that the respective tribal names were written on them. So far, nothing could indicate which staff would blossom.

41. Why should the people have known which staff would blossom? How does God's Word prove that we cannot know God's truth merely by human wisdom and judgment? How do Christians sometimes fail to understand and judge things spiritually, by God's Word alone?

42. How is the blossoming rod of Aaron a picture of Christ? How was Jesus vindicated and we with Him (see Romans 5; 1 Timothy 3:16)?

Public Ministry: God's Gift to His People

Read chapters 18 and 19. God vindicated the house of Aaron. Only they were chosen to approach Him in the sanctuary (Numbers 8:19; 16:5; 18:3–4, 22). Because of this vindication, the people became aware of their unholy condition (contrast with Numbers 16:3) and the mortal danger it put them in if they came near the tabernacle (17:12). God's presence now meant for them wrath, judgment, and death.

However, God's presence and the tabernacle existed among them for the very opposite reason: to save them from their sin and its horrible consequences. The priesthood was God's *gift* to them (18:7). Through the priestly service of the house of Aaron, the people were saved from judgment (v. 5), and the nation remained in communion with God (vv. 6–7).

43. How does Christ fulfill the Old Testament priesthood, and why, through faith alone, do we partake of its saving reality?

44. How is the tabernacle both Law and Gospel? How is the tabernacle's saving purpose known only after we recognize that by it we're condemned by God's Law?

Strangely enough, in a sense, it is by holy Aaron being made unholy ("you shall bear iniquity," v. 1) that the unholy people were spared wrath and blessed by the Lord.

45. Who is it that ultimately takes responsibility for our sin? How has this been done once and for all, and how is that saving reality made known and brought to us? How do all true Christians live this way in Christ?

The priestly class (the Levites) in Israel relied upon divine authority and power for its institution. Unlike the Gentile nations around them, the priests could not own and hold land, a powerful political and social mechanism for wielding control.

In contrast, the Levites had no inheritance except God (Numbers 18:20; 26:62). They lived among the tribes in 48 small settlements (34:16–35:6; Joshua 13–21). Their "income" was derived from the offerings and gifts of the people (tithes, firstfruits, and food of the altar).

46. Although Christ has fulfilled the Law and paid our tithe or our debt to the temple (see Matthew 17:24–27), how does the principle of support for the public Office of Ministry apply today? How are the Levites also typical of all believers?

The gifts and offerings appointed by the Lord were for the benefit of the Levites. The Levites were God's gift to the people to perform the necessary work for their salvation and blessing. This is what God truly desired for them. Consequently, their tithes, their firstfruits, and all the substance of what they gave were, in fact, not for the Lord but for their poor and needy brothers the Levites (though it was done "as unto the Lord"). The gifts of the altar were then offered by the Levite, whose they were now. So, it was by *the priest's* sacrifice of what was now *his* substance, that atonement was made on behalf of the worshiper.

47. For whom does Christ desire we make our gifts and offerings? How does the Gospel teach us to value, cherish, and support

the public ministry? Why is withholding support for the public ministry on account of the personal weaknesses, imperfections, or faults of those who serve in it a rejection of Christ?

Read chapter 19. God's gift of the Levitical service and the bounty of God's grace that it delivered to God's people are seen in the unusual cleansing water provided to make pure anyone defiled in any way. The normal rituals of cleansing required making sacrifice (see Leviticus 14:10; 15:13, 28), which could be expensive. The number of times in the normal course of a day or week when someone might become unclean was so high, and the price of the sacrifice required was so great, that people found it impossible to keep the Law. However, God's mercy provides what people cannot. An unblemished red heifer (cow) was burnt whole outside the camp (with cedarwood, hyssop, and scarlet yarn thrown unto the fire). These ashes were then reserved outside the camp for use in special cleansing water that accomplished what otherwise required altar sacrifices to be brought by the unclean.

48. How did the red heifer speak of Christ? How do we see in this Christian Baptism?

Unbelief: The Peril of Despising Means of Grace

Read 20:1–13. The people were once again complaining to Moses about a lack of water and accusing him of misleading God's people. Moses seeks the Lord's counsel and is told to gather the people to the rock, with staff in hand and Aaron at his side, and to tell the rock "to yield its water" (20:8). Instead, Moses strikes the rock twice and water pours forth.

Moses made use of means other than that appointed by God and disobeyed the Lord. Consequently, God tells him that his unbelief has forfeited him entrance into the land.

49. What does Moses teach us about the vital importance of the means of grace? Is anyone above the Word of God? Does Moses prove

himself no different than those whom he called “rebels” (see Numbers 27:14)?

50. In 1 Corinthians 10:4, we are told that the rock from which the people drank (both here and in Exodus 17:1–6) was Christ. How is this so, and how does a comparison of both incidents show us Christ and the difference between Law and Gospel?

In Closing

Encourage participants to begin the following activities:

- Read 2 Timothy 3:15–16 and discuss the sufficiency of God’s Word and its power in our lives.
- Have class members discuss ways in which we are tempted to do God’s work by human means.
- Read 20:14–21:3 to prepare for the next session.

Close with prayer.

Lesson 6

Death and Destruction

Following the tragic failure of Moses at the waters of Meribah, the Israelites completed their forty years of wandering. It was time to commence the third leg of their journey and travel from Kadesh to the plains of Moab (Numbers 22:1).

Read 20:14–21:3. In this lesson, we will see that as the journey heads toward the Promised Land, more death lay in the path of the people. They will learn that in their earthly pilgrimage of faith, life is had in the midst of death. God is the only source, hope, and true life; all else, being corrupted by sin, is but death.

Denial Is Not Delay

A direct route to their destination required Israel to pass through a portion of the land controlled by the nation of Edom. Moses sent a delegation to the King of Moab with a plea to allow them passage. The Israelites gave diplomatic assurances that the people, numbering in the millions, would not use up the natural resources of the land. They would make their way along what is likely a common trade route, the King's Highway (20:14–17).

Edom flatly refused. As a result, Israel took a more circuitous route, likely along the border (Numbers 21:4).

51. What is the significance of Israel calling itself Edom's "brother" (20:14)? What bearing does this have on Israel's decision not to invade as it does other nations?

52. How do you suppose the people of Israel felt about Moses, or even the Lord, considering this delay? How do we react when our plans are rerouted or when we encounter delays?

53. Read 20:14–16. What does Israel's suffering and their deliverance by God's mercy tell the Edomites about them? Is such an appeal compelling? How are our lives as Christians the same in this world?

The Death of Aaron

Read 20:22–29. One notable death has already occurred, that of Miriam, the sister of Moses and Aaron (20:1). However, when the people settle at Mount Hor, God reveals that it is time for Aaron to die. Aaron is reminded that he will be denied entrance into the land because with Moses he sinned against the Lord in unbelief.

Aaron's son, Eleazar, will succeed him. God commanded Moses to take Aaron and his son up Mount Hor in the sight of all the people and there remove Aaron of his Levitical vestments and place them on Eleazar.

Aaron remained there to die and to be buried. So great was his death that "all the house of Israel wept for Aaron thirty days" (20:29).

54. With Moses' and Aaron's failure came an end to Aaron's priesthood. How is this theologically significant? How does this show the impossibility of righteousness by the Law? (See Romans 8:1–3; Hebrews 7:12.)

55. How does the transfer of garments from Aaron to Eleazar portray salvation? Are both Law and Gospel evident? Where do we find this portrayed for us in our worship?

56. Although there is joy over God's provision of a continuing priesthood for their salvation, Israel nevertheless mourned the death of

Aaron. Does this depict the life of faith in this world? Is there both sorrow and joy in death? How is this so in our worship of Christ?

The Church Militant

Conflict was not something new to the people of Israel. With God's help, they had previously fought and won (Exodus 17:8–15). However, their recent experience of failure due to unbelief (Numbers 14:41–45) taught them that without faith in the Lord, they would be doomed to defeat.

God had fought for Israel and defeated Pharaoh and all Egypt (Exodus 14:14). He would do likewise in all their battles so that Israel could take land that God had promised them (Deuteronomy 1:30). The enemies of the Lord must be defeated in battle, routed by Him through His people. Israel was not to accommodate these warring nations and kingdoms, but was to oppose and destroy them (21:2).

A Canaanite king of a large city called Arad, apparently attempted to overtake or surprise them through "the way of Atharim," (21:2). The word *Atharim* may refer to either a geographical region with a well-known caravan road or a clandestine route taken by spies and bandits (some Hebrew texts have a spelling for *Atharim* that means "spies"). The king managed to abscond with hostages whom he held prisoner, doubtless as pawns with which he would negotiate some sort of surrender or peace with Israel.

Israel's response was one of courageous faith that will not be intimidated, but will make the place "holy" in the way that God desires—by devoting it to destruction.

57. In what ways do Christians sometimes forget their call to spiritual warfare in this world? How are we tempted to give in? What kinds of threats does the devil use to frighten us into submission?

58. Why is this place called "Hormah" (Numbers 21:3)?

59. How does the previous event of Aaron's death tie into this?

In Closing

Encourage participants to begin the following activities:

- Ask participants to share their devotional piety (prayers, worship attendance, and so on) on Good Friday.
- Discuss the nature of spiritual conflict.
- Read Numbers 21:1–22:1 to prepare for the next session.

Close with prayer.

Lesson 7

Look and Live

As Israel continues her journey to the plains of Moab, she is learning that God's grace alone sustains her. In this section (21:1–22:1), we see that Israel's faith continues to grow. Israel is nurtured as God faithfully provides for His people, and, in one campaign after another, He delivers Israel and gives her victory in battle.

The narrative begins with a dramatic episode of divine chastisement involving "fiery serpents" (Numbers 21:6). These bite the people with a deadly venom until God provides a strange remedy (21:4–9). Following this, a diary of sorts notes several stopping places along the way (21:10–20). This concludes with Israel's conquest of two Amorite kings, Sihon and Og (21:21–35).

Killing Sin with Sin

Being denied passage through Edomite territory, Israel was forced to skirt the southern border in the desert. With this delay, the people grew impatient and lapsed back into their old ways of complaining. God and Moses were the objects of their criticism. The manna was described as "worthless food," and God's purpose seemed to be one of suffering and death (21:4–5).

60. Did Israel recognize God's provision and purpose on their behalf? Why is faith necessary? How are God's ways hidden to us in circumstances and events?

61. Do we ever consider the manna of the Gospel to be "worthless" (21:5)? (See also Psalm 78:24–25; 105:40; John 6:31.)

As punishment for their defiance, God sent "fiery serpents" to bite the people. Their lethal venom brought death to "many people" (21:6–7).

The people asked Moses to intercede once more. In a merciful response, God directed Moses to craft the likeness of a fiery serpent and place it on a pole so that whoever looked at it would not die. Moses fashioned one from bronze fastened it to a pole, and erected this image so that all could see the bronze serpent lifted up and live.

Read John 3, especially verses 13–21. Note how the lifting up of the serpent by Moses is said to foreshadow Christ's crucifixion.

62. In what ways does the bronze serpent lifted up by Moses signify Christ's death upon the cross?

63. How is sin turned into salvation, and cursing into blessing? Why is this possible through the cross of Jesus Christ?

64. Discuss why faith alone saves. What is the promise being held forth in the bronze serpent?

Songs of Thankfulness and Praise

Israel has grown in their experience of God's mysterious ways. He has proven Himself to be a God that "no eye has seen, nor ear heard, nor the heart of man imagined" (1 Corinthians 2:9; Isaiah 64:4). He cannot be tracked or traced, except through faith alone guided by His Word of promise alone. Israel has been learning to live by God's mercy and grace. They see how precarious human life is without His gifts. God has been good to these sinners.

Their journeys continue, taking them from Oboth to Iye-abarim, from there to the valley of Zered, and then on to the other side of the Arnon (River). In effect, their route had them marching in a circle around Moab and Edom. God makes His people victorious one way or another. This is memorialized in verse as a witness to God's saving grace for His people (21:14–15).

65. Read 2 Corinthians 2:14. How does faith—resting on God's Word of promise in Christ—assure us of victory no matter which route our lives may take? Why may we be jubilant in the wanderings of faith?

Pressing ahead, the Lord tells Moses to gather the people to Beer, meaning "well." This is the place where the Lord will provide water for His people. In remembrance of this, another canticle is composed. Although its meaning is somewhat obscure, this canticle praises God for the provision of water from wells dug out for use by a royal house. Israel is God's prince and His royal people, and, therefore, He has prepared these wells for them (21:16–18).

66. How does the preparation of these wells through the hands of another—a king—portray Christ and God's grace in our lives?

67. Where in the Divine Service do we celebrate God's provision for our lives in a similar manner?

The Fight of Faith

This portion of our lesson closes out with the defeat of two Amorite Kings, Sihon and Og of Bashan. In both cases, the kingdoms are decimated, and Israel takes "possession" of the land (21:24, 35).

68. Read 2 Corinthians 10:1–6. To what extent are the claims of Christ's lordship over our lives?

69. In verse 34, God directs us, "Do not fear him." Is this message one of Law or Gospel? How does it operate?

In Closing

Encourage participants to begin the following activities:

- Have students recall spiritually significant times in their lives.
- Study John 3:13–21 more closely.
- Read chapters 22–25 to prepare for the next session.

Close with prayer.

Lesson 8

Balak, Balaam, and Baal

Trusting in God, Israel has seen that the will and power of their enemies, however determined and resourceful, cannot prevail against them. God has promised to bring them into the land, and He will keep His Word.

A new kind of force, however, is used against them. Read chapters 22 through 25. Up until now, Israel has faced mere flesh and blood. Now, though, dark spiritual forces are summoned in order to bring misfortune upon them and to curse them on their way. Balak, the Moabite king, is threatened by Israel's presence. (Interestingly, Israel is now inspiring fear in others, and not the other way around; see 22:2). Balak calls for a famous seer named Balaam, who is known for his effectiveness as a sorcerer (22:6).

After repeated offers of generous remuneration, Balaam agrees to the King's request to pronounce a curse upon Israel. Balaam, by means of his pagan augury and evil divination, inquires of the God of Israel, whom he knows to be named Yahweh ("the LORD," 23:3). God previously revealed to Balaam that the Israelites were a people blessed by Him. Balaam told King Balak that he could only speak what God placed in his mouth (22:28). Through these forbidden means, though, he attempts to conjure and manipulate God in a way that will bring the desired results. Each time Balaam prophesies, he gives an oracle favorable to the children of Israel.

Balaam does this three times before seeing that his spiritism and occult powers cannot overcome the Lord God of Israel (24:1). Then, he utters his final oracle, which again imparts a benediction to Israel, ending with the promise made to Abraham centuries before (24:9; see Genesis 12:2–3).

Balaam is clearly a tool of Satan, who, by spiritual artifice, works to destroy God's people. So when opposition from the outside does not work, he resorts to an attack from within. In chapter 25, Balaam plots to infect the Israelites with strange gods through carnal union with Moabite women and syncretistic worship in the temples of their gods.

There is much we do not have time to examine, so our lessons will center around three main aspects of the narrative: the character of Balaam; his oracles and how God's Word trumps them; and, finally, the unionism and syncretism of the Israelites with the Baal of Peor.

A Mercenary Ministry

Balaam is essentially a prophet for hire. He is a professional seer or sorcerer (Joshua 13:22) whose ministry has its price. He is mentioned in an extrabiblical text dating around 800 BC (see Gordon J. Wenham, *Exploring the Old Testament: A Guide to the Pentateuch, Volume 1* [InterVarsity Press: Downers Grove, Illinois, 2003], p. 115). Balaam has mastered spiritual forces and offers his services for his own advantage and gain. Read the New Testament's commentary on Balaam in 2 Peter 2:15, Jude 1:11, and Revelation 2:14.

70. What do these passages say about Balaam and his ministry? Where does the narrative from Numbers confirm this?

71. How does Balaam differ from a true prophet? Contrast Moses with Balaam.

72. How is God's hidden work with Balaam to be rightly understood? Does this legitimize false religion?

73. Discuss the subtlety of Balaam's unionistic tactic and why it was expedient for him to adopt the name of the Lord while not really believing in Him. How does he make use of incrementalism to corrupt the faith of God's people (see Numbers 31:16)?

Cursing Turned to Blessing

Balaam's first three discourses, or oracles, follow a pattern. He offers sacrifices to God from what is thought to be a spiritually strategic location. To the great dismay of King Balak, however, instead of cursing Israel each time, Balaam blesses them. Moses, in his final words, reminds Israel of God's mercy in doing this (Deuteronomy 23:5). This is also noted a thousand years later (Nehemiah 13:2).

God's mercy is evident beforehand in the incident of Balaam's donkey (22:21–34). Balaam traveled to Balak by God's permission (22:20), but the donkey turned aside from the road three times. On each occasion, Balaam beat the donkey. It is revealed that the lowly beast is saving Balaam's sinful life (22:33) from the angel of the Lord, who stood in their path with the sword of destruction (22:22, 24, 26). The donkey speaks and declares its faithfulness to Balaam, who has shown no appreciation for what she has done (22:28–30).

74. Is the donkey a picture of Christ? If so, how? What lesson is taught to Balaam through her actions?

In his oracles, Balaam declares Israel to be a people not "cursed," separate from the nations, and "righteous" (23:7–10). He further pronounces them "blessed" (23:20), as those in whom God has seen no "misfortune" or "trouble" (23:21), probably referring to sin or iniquity. So great is their deliverance that no divination can succeed against Israel (23:22). God's Word is what prevails (24:19), so that although Balaam intends to curse, it is God's blessing that is spoken (see Matthew 5:11; Luke 6:21–23).

75. On what basis is this said of God's people (see Galatians 3:3–13)? How are the powers of darkness to which humans are enslaved by nature (see Ephesians 2:1–2; Hebrews 2:15) made powerless by God (see Psalm 68:18; Ephesians 4:8; Colossians 2:15)?

76. Ultimately, of whom are the words in 24:5–9 speaking?

Balaam's last oracle (24:15–24) foretells of a scepter that will rise out of Israel, a "star" from Israel that will destroy Moab, Edom, Amalek, the Kenites, Asshur, and Eber. (Note verse 14 and the words "in the latter days.")

77. Read Matthew 2:1–11. Could this prophecy be that of which the magi spoke?

Baal of Peor

What Balaam could not accomplish through open opposition, he could gain through infiltration and corrupting influence from within (Numbers 31:16). If God could not be turned against His people, Balaam would turn God's people against Him. This was done through encouraging a blending of the religious worship of Israel with that of the Moabites. This is syncretism and unionism.

The result was sexual immorality being practiced with "the daughters of Moab" (25:1) and the worship of false gods (25:2). These are likely temple prostitutes of the fertility god Baal-Peor. The Israelites are willingly led to believe that through sexual union with these women they can secure a good harvest and agricultural prosperity. Balaam may have won the confidence of the Israelites by claiming his oracles as proof of his approval as a minister of God.

God ordered the hanging of every "chief of the people" (25:4). Moses did not obey God, however, and a plague ensued killing twenty-four thousand people. The plague was stopped because of the faith of a priest named Phinehas, who spears Zimri (a Simeonite leader) and the woman he took into his tent, Cozbi, daughter of a Midian chief (25:6–17).

78. Why has Moses been largely absent from this part of the narrative? What does his failure to obey God say to us (see 25:5)?

79. How does this lesson apply to us (see Revelation 2:14, 20)?

In Closing

Encourage participants to begin the following activities:

- Read Matthew 7:15; 24:11, 24; Luke 6:26; 2 Peter 2:1; 1 John 4:1.
- Describe the characteristics of false prophets.
- Read Numbers 26:1–30:16 to prepare for the next session.

Close with prayer.

Lesson 9

The Second Census and Instructions

Israel was situated just across the Jordan, with Jericho on the other side (Joshua 2:1). Final preparations must be made for their entrance into Canaan. This lesson takes a look at how God continued to ready His people for their inheritance in the land (26:1–30:16).

These chapters mainly address the following: the second census and preparation for inheritance (26:1–27:11); the commission of Joshua as Moses' successor (27:12–23); and worship by sacrifice (28–30).

The Second Census

Read chapter 26. Nearly forty years before, the first census was taken. The first census primarily provided enlistment rosters for war and a means by which the Levitical tribe could be organized for its service (see chapter 1). More military conflict lay ahead, though (25:16–18). After so many losses and gains through the years (the tribe of Simeon has lost 37,100 people, and Manasseh has grown by 20,500), a fresh start is needed.

However, the second census also serves as a basis for apportioning the land and dividing it as inheritance among the twelve tribes, save the Levites (26:52–56, 62).

80. Compare the total of this census, 601,730 (26:51), with that thirty-nine years prior, 603,550 (1:46).What does this say about God's faithfulness to multiply Abraham's descendants (see Genesis 12:2–3)?

81. Read 26:8–10. What warning do we read about here? Why does this mean we must trust in but may not presume the grace of God?

In 27:1–11, the daughters of a man named Zelophehad appeal to Moses for the right of inheritance. By custom, inheritance is transmitted to the male seed of a household, with the firstborn receiving the largess of the goods (Deuteronomy 21:15–17). A daughter could receive gifts in her dowry, but upon marriage all her property became part of the assets of her husband's estate. God decrees, however, that in Israel land titles may be passed on to daughters in the case of a man who has no sons. Later, it is stipulated that such women must marry within their tribe in order that no land be transferred from one tribe to another (Numbers 36:1–12).

82. How is this rule of land inheritance a lesson of grace? Consider how this is followed by a reminder of Moses' rebellion that forfeited his entering the land (27:14). What Law/Gospel contrast is evident here?

Joshua (Jesus): The New Moses

A new leader must be provided to take God's people into the Promised Land and rid it of the "seven nations" (Deuteronomy 7:1). Moses disqualified himself through his unbelief (failing to "uphold [God] as holy in the eyes of the people of Israel," Numbers 20:12).

Moses asks God to appoint a leader in his place who will "go out before them and come in before them, who shall lead them out and bring them in, that the congregation of the LORD may not be as sheep that have no shepherd" (27:17).

83. Read Ezekiel 34:8–19, Matthew 9:36, and John 10:1–18. How does Joshua typify Christ?

Joshua has been Moses' faithful servant, doing as he said, being a witness to the Word of God, and joining him on his ascent of Mount Sinai (Exodus 17:9–10, 14; 24:13). He has shown himself to be a man of faith. Along with Caleb, Joshua was the last of the previous generation to enter the land (Numbers 14:38; 26:65).

In fact, Joshua was more righteous than even Moses! This is suggested in Exodus 33:7–11. There, we are told that Moses entered the Tent of Meeting (the tabernacle) in order to speak with God "face to face" (Exodus 33:11). No one was allowed to enter or come near the tabernacle except Moses and Aaron and his family. Yet, we are told that Joshua, Moses' assistant, is stationed at the tent and remained there even after Moses had left (Exodus 33:11: "Joshua . . . would not depart from the tent," suggesting he was actually inside). How this can be without his being struck dead is remarkable in the extreme.

84. What does this say about Joshua and God's grace in his life? Read Hebrews 4:8 and 10:18. Where does the true Joshua lead us and why is His ministry better than that of Moses?

Worship by Sacrifice

In the Old Testament, God instituted a system of sacrifice to make His people holy purely by His grace. Because of the perversity of sin, because of its temporal causes and its eternal consequences, sacrifice had to be made. However, the animal life and agricultural produce offered in sacrifice were exceedingly costly.

85. Read Psalm 40:6–8 and Hebrews 10:5–10. How do the appointed sacrifices in Israel help us to appreciate the inestimable value of Christ's sacrifice, which is their fulfillment?

86. Why is this necessary to prepare God's people for living in the land? How does faith in Christ accomplish this in our lives?

87. Read chapter 30. Notice the strict binding of the law of vows. Can we make such vows to God? How is this, in fact, a picture of God's own faithfulness to us despite our sinfulness?

In Closing

Encourage participants to begin the following activities:

- Study in depth John 10:1–30.
- Share their thoughts on what Christ's sacrifice means to them.
- Read Numbers 31–32 to prepare for the next session.

Close with prayer.

Lesson 10

War and Settlement

This lesson covers the war and plunder of the Midianites by Israel as commanded by God (31:1–21). The spoils of war are divided among the Israelites, with portions set aside for the Levites (31:25–54). Finally, the desire of the tribes of Reuben and Gad to settle in this area is recorded, with Moses pledging them to faithfulness in the conquest of the land across the Jordan (chapter 32).

The Lord's Retribution

The Midianites (a particular tribe of people among the larger ethnic body designated as Moabites) had not merely resisted or opposed Israel, but had attempted by stealth and seduction to overthrow the very name of God. Theirs was an especially heinous and diabolical act for which God issued a stern edict of vengeance to be carried out against them by Israel (33:1).

One thousand warriors from each tribe were sent into battle (31:4–6). With Eleazar the high priest and Phinehas leading them, along with "vessels of the sanctuary," they warred against the Midianites killing every male (v. 7), every royal person (v. 8), and set fire to every town, village, and city (v. 10).

88. Why do you suppose God reveals His wrath so terribly against the Midianites? Read Romans 16:17–18; 2 Corinthians 6:14–18; and Jude 1:3–4. What is God's attitude toward the compromise of doctrine and syncretistic worship?

89. Are we called, in effect, to wage war against the world? In what way is Baptism a decimation of the world of sin (see Galatians 5:24; 6:14; Ephesians 4:22–24)?

At first, only the adult males were killed. However, seeing that the very women and younger men (likely temple prostitutes of both genders) who insinuated their evil ways into the hearts of God's people remained alive, Moses ordered all of them killed (31:13–18). He permitted only virgins to remain alive; that is, he spared those who had not been adulterated or defiled in this way.

90. Read 1 Corinthians 6:13–20. Discuss how sexual sin, especially fornication, stains lives in terrible ways and why illicit sexual union is singled out as a sin "against [one's] own body" (1 Corinthians 6:18). How might this play in the decision to annihilate the Midianites defiled by their immoral religious practices?

The Plunder Divided

An equal division is made of the spoils of war between those who went to war and those who did not (31:25–27). The only difference was that the tribute levied on the soldiers was one five-hundredth (0.2 percent) of their portion (given to the priests), and the tribute of the people was one-fiftieth (2 percent) (given to the Levites; 31:28–31).

91. Read the following passages: John 15:15; 16:15; Romans 8:32; 1 Corinthians 3:21; Ephesians 1:3; Revelation 21:7. How much of God's wealth and bounty does Christ share with us? Where are these spoils handed out to us? Why does the fact that we receive them truly pay tribute to God?

In 31:48–54, military officers present Moses with jewelry made of gold and offer it as a sign of atonement. Not a single man was lost in the battle—God's grace was with them (v. 49)—and yet they sense their sinfulness and their indebtedness to God.

92. Read Romans 7:21–25. How does this text remind us that even in all our good works—done through faith alone—sin still dwells with us and we still need continual cleansing by the blood of Christ?

The Inheritance of Reuben and Gad

The tribes of Reuben and Gad make an astonishing request, to take as their inheritance the land of the Transjordan. This territory, situated above the Jordan Valley, is fertile and spacious, enjoying regular rainfall for crops and animals. It has fallen into Israel's possession, being taken from the Amorites (chapter 21) and the Midianites (chapter 31).

Moses is incensed and sees in this the same cowardice and treachery of unbelief by the ten spies (32:6–15). This is *not* the land God promised (see Numbers 34:1–12), and their request is disheartening the rest of the camp (32:7). He upbraids them for risking the possibility of being denied entrance for another forty years since they might refuse to enter the land with the other tribes, thereby destroying their spiritual unity of faith.

93. Is the Christian Church divided in similar ways? What kinds of false ambitions, worldly glory, or sectarian interests interfere with the unity that comes only through a common faith?

94. Why do you suppose God permits this? Does the promise of Reuben and Gad to cross the Jordan and join the tribes in battle persuade God to do so (32:33–34)? Read Joshua 4:12 and 22:1–6 and see how these tribes kept their word.

In Closing

Encourage participants to begin the following activities:

- Read Genesis 37–42 and be familiar with the patriarch Reuben.
- Read Joshua 22. Discuss why Reuben, Gad, and the half tribe of Manasseh built an altar to the Lord.
- Read Numbers 33:1–36:13 to prepare for the next session.

Close with prayer.

Lesson 11

Review and Regulations

In these final chapters, 33 through 36, the narrative closes out with a summary of the past and plans for the future. While faith is always looking forward, it does so as it is taught lessons of sin and grace from the past. Chapter 33 is a rehearsal of Israel's experience from the Exodus until now, with a word of exhortation added. Chapters 34 through 36 concern life in the land, establishing territorial borders for the nation and naming the official surveyors for the tribe. The provision is made for special cities of refuge, and additional inheritance regulations are given.

95. Read Romans 15:4 and 1 Corinthians 10:1–14. Does God mean for us to learn from the past?

Love Does Not Keep Account of Wrongs

Read 33:1–49. Besides mentioning the places where Israel camped along the way, this passage says very little. Only the Exodus is given elaboration. Otherwise, only a few brief notations (vv. 9, 14, 38–40) are made of Israel's forty years.

It is striking that Israel's sins and failures are not mentioned. It is as if God were blind to all they did. Certainly, this is not because no record has been made of their misdeeds (see Deuteronomy 1–3). Yet, God's account here suggests that this story is not about their unfaithfulness but about His faithfulness.

96. Is this the way God sees our lives (see 1 Corinthians 4:5; 2 Corinthians 4:17–18; Galatians 2:20; Colossians 3:3)?

God commanded Israel to engage in what is called *total war* against the inhabitants of the land. This is the unqualified decimation of those civilizations, complete with the razing of all structures, and the total obliteration of their cultures, especially any element of their idolatrous religion.

This is not new to them but a reiteration of previous instructions (see Exodus 23:20–33; 34:11–17; Leviticus 20:1–9).

97. Why was this destruction just and necessary? What objections might be raised to this policy? How is Baptism similar to this as it pertains to our sinful nature (see Romans 6:1–7; 8:13; 2 Corinthians 7:1; Colossians 3:5; Hebrews 7–10; 1 Peter 3:18)?

Holy Land

Borders of the land are given in Numbers 34:1–15. Four times, this territory is described as their inheritance (vv. 2, 13–15).

98. How does viewing the land as a gift make a difference in their regard for it? Read Romans 8:29, Galatians 3:16, and Hebrews 1:2. Who is the true and final heir of this land and of all things?

Moses appointed certain chiefs from each tribe under the direction of Joshua and Eleazar to determine the allotments of land to each tribe (and clans within the tribe).

99. Read Matthew 20:21–23. Who determines our portion in God's kingdom? Is it on the basis of our purpose-driven works or does God determine it according to His grace?

Holy Living

Special cities are appointed to be built in Israel for the sake of the Levites (35:1–8). There are forty-eight in all, with six of these cities designated as "cities of refuge" (v. 6). Three of these on one side of the Jordan and three on the other (v. 14).

The size of these "cities" tells us they are more like small settlements or hamlets. The surrounding pastures extended beyond the town limits by 2,000 cubits (approximately 1,000 yards) in each direction (35:4–5).

100. How does this portray the Christian Church? What should be the peaceful and joyful spiritual life of congregations?

In the cities of refuge, anyone guilty of manslaughter could flee if pursued by an accuser or someone seeking revenge. The high priest afforded him or her sanctuary until the time of trial, and even then if found innocent the accused was obligated to live in the Levitical city until the high priest died (v. 28). This law was also meant to prevent defilement of the land since it was God's dwelling place, as well (v. 34). The land was kept pure by the spilling of blood (either the execution of the accused, if found guilty, or the sacrifices offered up by the priests), just as the spilling of blood defiled it.

101. How is Christ portrayed in these places of refuge (see Ephesians 2:12–19)?

Finally, a law was established that forbade intertribal marriage and the transfer of hereditary estates from one tribe to another (36:1–12). This law was warranted by the marriage of female heirs. The inheritance was God's permanent gift that, by His grace, belonged to those to whom He gave it. Therefore, the law kept in check the ambitions of more prosperous tribes to enlarge themselves and through acquisitive maneuvers to gain control of larger territory. The lust for power and the tendency of self-aggrandizement were inhibited by God's gracious arrangement.

Through faith in Christ, we have the promise of an inheritance that we cannot lose or have taken from us. We may be content with the life that God has given us since His grace has blessed us in all things (Philippians 4:11; Hebrews 13:5).

102. Read Matthew 5:19–20, 19:29, and 25:34. Why may we be content with this life? How does the promise of an eternal inheritance assure us of God's good will toward us in Christ?

In Closing

Encourage participants to begin the following activities:

- Read Proverbs 10:12 and 1 Peter 4:8.
- Consider how we tend to see past the faults of those we love.

Close with prayer.

Leader Notes

These notes are provided as a safety net, a place to turn for help in answering questions and for enriching discussion. They will not answer every question raised in your class. Please read them, along with the questions, before class. Consult them in class only after exploring the Bible references and discussing what they teach. Please note the different abilities of your class members. Some will easily find the Bible passages listed in this study; others will struggle. To make participation easier, team up members of the class. For example, if a question asks you to look up several passages, assign one passage to one group, the second to another, and so on. Divide the work! Let participants present the answers they discover.

Preparing to Teach Numbers

To prepare to lead this study, read through the Book of Numbers. You might read the introduction to the Book of Numbers in the *Concordia Self-Study Bible* or a Bible handbook. Several maps showing the Old Testament world around the time of Moses (ca. 1526 BC and later) would also be helpful.

The materials in these notes are designed to help you in leading others through this portion of the Holy Scriptures. Nevertheless, this booklet is to be an aid to—and not a substitute for—your own study of and preparation for teaching the Book of Numbers.

If you have the opportunity, you will find it helpful to make use of other biblical reference works in the course of your study. These two commentaries can be very helpful: Gordon J. Wenham, *Numbers*, Tyndale Old Testament Commentaries (Downers Grove, Illinois: InterVarsity Press, 1981) and Paul W. Kuske, *Numbers*, People's Bible Commentary (Milwaukee: Northwestern Publishing House, 1990; reprinted by Concordia Publishing House, 2005). Although it is not strictly a commentary, the section on Numbers in *The Word Becoming Flesh* by Horace Hummel (St. Louis: Concordia Publishing House, 1979) also contains much that is of value for the proper interpretation of this biblical book.

Group Bible Study

Group Bible study means mutual learning from one another under the guidance of a leader. The Bible is an inexhaustible resource. No one person can discover all it has to offer. In a class, many eyes see many things and can apply them to many life situations. As the leader, you should resist the temptation to "give the answers" and so act as an "authority." This teaching approach stifles participation by individual members and can actually hamper learning. As a general rule the teacher is not to *give* interpretation but to *develop* interpreters. Of course there are times when you should and must share insights and information gained by your study and by your class members through the lesson. And you'll want to engage class members in meaningful sharing and discussion at all points, leading them to a summary of the lesson at the close. As a general rule, don't explain what the learners can discover by themselves.

Have a chalkboard and chalk or newsprint and marker available to emphasize significant points of the lesson. Rephrase your inquiries or the inquiries of participants as questions, problems, or issues. This provokes thought. Keep discussion to the point. List on the chalkboard or newsprint the answers given. Then determine the most vital points made in the discussion. Ask additional questions to fill gaps.

The aim of every Bible study is to help people grow spiritually, not merely in biblical and theological knowledge, but in Christian thinking and living. This means growth in Christian attitudes, insights, and skills for Christian living. The focus of this course must be the Church and the world of our day. The guiding question will be this: What does the Lord teach us for life today through the Book of Numbers?

Teaching the Old Testament

Teaching the Old Testament can degenerate into mere moralizing in which do-goodism becomes a substitute for the Gospel and sanctification gets confused with justification. Actually, the justified sinner is not moved by God's Law but by God's grace to a totally new life. His or her faith in Christ is always at work in every context of life. Meaningful personal Christianity consists of faith flowing from God's grace and is evidenced in love for other people. Having experienced God's free grace and forgiveness, the Christian daily works in his or her world to reflect the will of God for humanity in every area of human endeavor.

Christian leaders are Gospel oriented, not Law oriented. They distinguish between the two. Both Law and Gospel are needed. There is no clear Gospel unless we first have been crushed by the Law and see our sinfulness. There is no genuine Christianity where faith is not followed by a life pleasing to God. In fact, genuine faith is inseparable from life. The Gospel alone creates in us the new heart that causes us to love God and our neighbor.

When Christians teach the Old Testament, they do not teach it as a "law book," but instead as books containing both Law and Gospel. They see the God of the Old Testament as a God of grace who out of love establishes a covenant of love with His people (Deuteronomy 7:6–9) and forgives their sins. Christians interpret the Old Testament using the New Testament message of fulfilled prophecy through Jesus Christ. They teach as leaders who personally know the Lord Jesus as Savior, the victorious Christ who gives all believers a new life (2 Corinthians 5:17) and a new mission (John 20:21).

Pace Your Teaching

The lessons in this course of study are designed for a study session of at least an hour in length. If it is the desire and intent of the class to complete an entire lesson each session, it will be necessary for you to summarize the content of certain answers or biblical references in order to preserve time. Asking various class members to look up different Bible passages and to read them aloud to the rest of the class will save time over having every class member look up each reference.

Also, you may not want to cover every question in each lesson. This may lead to undue haste and frustration. Be selective. Pace your teaching. Spend no more than 5–10 minutes opening the lesson. During the lesson, get the sweep of meaning. Occasionally stop to help the class gain understanding of a word or concept. Allow approximately 5 minutes for closing the lesson and announcements.

Should your group have more than a one-hour class period, you can take it more leisurely. But do not allow any lesson to drag and become tiresome. Keep it moving. Keep it alive. Keep it meaningful. Eliminate some questions and restrict yourself to those questions most meaningful to the members of the class. If most members study the text at home, they can report their findings, and the time gained can be applied to relating the lesson to life.

Good Preparation

Good preparation by you, the leader, usually affects the pleasure and satisfaction the class will experience.

Suggestions to the Leader for Using the Study Guide

The Lesson Pattern

This set of lessons is designed to aid *Bible study*, that is, to aid a consideration of the written Word of God, with discussion and personal application growing out of the text at hand.

The typical lesson is divided into these sections:

1. Theme Verse
2. Objectives
3. Questions and Answers
4. Closing

The theme verse and objectives give you assistance in arousing the interest of the group in the concepts of the lesson. Here is where you stimulate minds of the class members. Do not linger too long over the introductory remarks.

The questions and answers provide the real spadework necessary for Bible study. Here the class digs, uncovers, and discovers; it gets the facts and observes them. Your comments are needed only to the extent that they help the group understand the text. The questions in this guide, corresponding to sections within the text, are intended to help the participants discover the meaning of the text.

Having determined what the text says, the class is ready to apply the message. Having heard, read, marked, and learned the Word of God, proceed to digest it inwardly through discussion, evaluation, and application. This is done, as this guide suggests, by taking the truths found in Scripture and applying them to the world and Christianity in general and then to personal Christian life. Class time may not permit discussion of all questions and topics. In preparation, you may need to select one or two and focus on them. Close the session by reviewing one important truth from the lesson.

Remember, the Word of God is sacred, but this study is not. The notes in this section offer only guidelines and suggestions. Do not hesitate to alter the guidelines or substitute others to meet your needs and the needs of the participants. Adapt your teaching plan to your class and your class period. Good teaching directs the learner to discover for himself or herself. For you, the teacher, this means directing the learner, not giving the learner answers. Choose the verses that should be looked up in Scripture. What discussion questions will you ask? At what points? Write them in the margin of your Study Guide. Involve class members, but give them clear directions. What practical actions might you propose for the week following the lesson? Which of the items do you consider most important for your class?

How will you best use your teaching period? Do you have 45 minutes? an hour? or an hour and a half? If time is short, what should you cut? Learn to become a wise steward of class time.

Be sure to take time to summarize the lesson, or have a class member do it. Plan a brief opening devotion, using members of the class.

Remember to pray frequently for yourself and your class. May God the Holy Spirit bless your study and your leading of others into the comforting truths of God's Christ-centered Word.

Lesson 1

The First Census of God's People

Theme verse: *The people of Israel shall pitch their tents . . . each man by his own standard. But the Levites shall camp around the tabernacle . . . that there may be no wrath on the congregation.*

Numbers 1:52–53

Objectives

By the power of the Holy Spirit working through God's Word, we will

- see how God acknowledges His people;
- appreciate our place as members of Christ's mystical body;
- strengthen our lives as members of God's royal priesthood;
- see Christ and learn how He is foreshadowed in Numbers.

1. The vital and basic difference between David's numbering of the people and that recorded in the Book of Numbers is that one was initiated by human pride and will (David's), and thus was an act of unbelief, and the other was initiated by the gracious will of God (Numbers), and thus was an act of faith.

In Numbers, God calls for the census not to make Israel proud or confident because of its size. This is a military census that marks out those eligible for service and provides a count of available troops. However, God's purpose was not to enable Israel to assess its strength and glory. God fights for His people, and He is their strength and glory.

Rather, this census is God's counting of the nation and an expression of His grace. Each member of the camp is acknowledged by God and given a place among God's people. He marks them out as the recipients of His grace, for whom He has promised to fight (Exodus 14:14). By doing so, God is encouraging them to trust in Him and not themselves. No matter their size, God has both numbered and named them as His own. That makes this census meaningful and pleasing in God's sight.

The narratives of 2 Samuel 24:1–17 and 1 Chronicles 21:1–17, on the other hand, reveal an act of wickedness. David is moved to number the people because of his pride. David does this not for national order, but for personal satisfaction and self-confidence ("that I may know the number of the people," 2 Samuel 24:2). He believed that by a human estimation and counting he could judge the nation and God's people.

The Christian Church also does this at times. While keeping records and statistics is a legitimate and God-pleasing work for good order and service to one another, when it becomes a means of judging ourselves as faithful or unfaithful, as blessed or not blessed, or when such numbering is made a standard of claiming to be spiritually healthy, strong, or growing, we have sinned against God.

2. Each of these warriors is a type of Christ. He is the true warrior who, on behalf of every nation, tribe, clan, family, and person, fought the enemies of humankind—sin, death, hell, and the devil—and prevailed against them for our salvation (Revelation 3:21; 12:11).

Jesus is our conquering Redeemer, the captain or leader of our salvation (Hebrews 5:9). He has overcome this sinful world and its hostile powers of spiritual darkness for us. In John 16:33, He tells us to "take heart" in knowing that this is so.

Christ's victory is given to us through the Gospel, in Baptism and in the Lord's Supper, and is received through faith alone. Growing strong in the Lord is not a matter of acquiring, earning, or somehow "working up" more grace. It is learning to put on Christ through faith more deeply and consistently each day. We live confidently and trustingly in our Baptism as God's promise that, for Christ's sake, we have been delivered from sin and death and made His heirs (Galatians 3:27; Ephesians 6:11).

3. Liberal critics scoff at the coincidence of census totals as impossible. They insist this demonstrates an artificial character of Scripture that is evidence of editorial tampering that may be found throughout the Bible.

Because critics know that the integrity of the biblical text is unassailable, they must go beyond it with radical and unbelieving criticisms that are built upon supposition and conjecture.

The faithful and believing hearer of God's Word sees in this a divine witness from God. He knows His people and preserves them in His grace. Not one of them is lost, as Jesus said (John 17:12). Though this particular work of providence (identical tallies) occurs rarely, it is a testimony to us that when numbers do not add up, when things seem lost and God's people forgotten, they really are not.

4. In Revelation 7:1–8 and 14:1–5, God's people are symbolically portrayed as 144,000 of "the sons of Israel." There are twelve thousand from each tribe (Joseph stands in place of Ephraim, and Dan is dropped from the list). In chapter 7, they are said to be sealed by God on their foreheads. We are told in 14:1 that this is "His [the Lamb's or Christ's] name and His Father's." They are situated with Christ on Mount Zion (the Zion above, Hebrews 12:22), where they learn, and apparently sing, a new song of redemption, which they alone know. They are further described as virgins who "follow the Lamb wherever He goes," and are the firstfruits of redemption. They are said to be true witnesses ("in their mouth is no lie") and "blameless" (Revelation 14:4–5).

All of these are metaphors of God's grace in Christ, which has qualified sinners to be God's people. Just as God's choosing of Israel and endowing people with natural health and strength qualified them for service, so in Christ we have been made fit for God and His kingdom. His Spirit was poured out upon us in Baptism, and with the forgiveness of sins imparts a divine newness to our lives that is expressed in our faith. This sounds in God's ears like a beautiful, heavenly song. Likewise, having Christ as our redeeming Lord means that our lives and His are one. Where we are He is, and where He is we are. This is possible by God's grace alone and is what we receive through faith alone.

However, our salvation is not necessarily evident to the human eye. By and large, it remains hidden under the external forms of lives that appear sinful, weak, sad, impure, and forsaken. God knows who His people are, though, and they are marked by the Gospel and faith. Where the Gospel is preached and where the Sacraments are rightly administered there, despite how few and how outwardly inglorious, are God's chosen people. Before Him they are not condemned (they are "blameless"), but are forever blessed and pleasing in His sight for Christ's sake.

5. In Numbers 1:47–54, we are told that the Levites are exempted from the military census because their responsibilities concerned the tabernacle and its services. They will be counted shortly in another two-part census exclusively for them.

This shows how God appoints only some and not all of His people for public service. From the beginning of time, God has served

His people. In original creation prior to the fall, He did so directly, communing with Adam and Eve in the garden. He did this to reveal His gracious and holy character, generously providing this service for their benefit and blessing.

After the fall, God's grace continued, but through appointed representatives who, in His name, would act to serve God's people for their salvation. No person had the right to perform this service simply by being a believer. Later in Israel's history, King Saul would learn the disastrous consequences of arrogating to himself the service of the priesthood without a call (1 Samuel 13:8–14).

Likewise in the Christian Church, though all are servants, not all are public ministers. To be sure, all Christians, as the Church together, are given the keys of the kingdom and the power to remit and retain sins. However, by Christ's mandate, the public use of these keys and exercise of this power are to be done regularly, ordinarily, and normally only by called and ordained men. Exceptional cases, such as emergency Baptism or private consolation where absolution may be assured, are not in view, of course. However, no Christian in the name of his or her royal priesthood may presume regularly to perform the services of public ministry for which Christ instituted the Pastoral Office (see Matthew 28:19–20).

6. The Levitical duties layed out in 1:50–51 include the erecting, taking down, transport, and care of the tabernacle and all its furnishings. The Levites also had to set up their personal tent dwellings immediately around the tabernacle as a barrier in order to prevent its sanctity from being violated. This buffer zone, as it were, stationed the Levites where it would be evident to all that this is where none shall pass without submission to Levitical cleansing.

The "wrath" mentioned in verse 53 refers to the fact that by their daily service at the brazen altar, in the courtyard, and in the tabernacle as they made offering for sin and carried out the ceremonial laws of worship, the Levites kept the nation holy. Of course, these ministrations were not a matter of works, but services instituted wholly by grace because they were types and shadows of Christ. In time, though, faith in God's grace was replaced by self-righteous legalism.

Hebrews says that Christ is the true tabernacle that "the Lord set up, not man" (8:2), one "not made with hands" (9:11). The Levitical priesthood was inferior to Christ's, which Hebrews says is "after the order of Melchizedek" (5:6, 10; 6:20; 7:11, 17). Christ's service endures forever since He lives eternally, unlike the Levitical services.

The Levites died and with them all their works (7:16, 23–24). Jesus offered Himself up once for all (9:12, 26; 10:10) to take away God's wrath (Isaiah 53:1–12) so that now in Him there is no condemnation (Romans 8:1). Through Christ we have free and full access into God's gracious presence at every moment (Hebrews 10:14–23). There is no need to "build up" holy structures and fear God's wrath for our sin so long as we look to Christ as the true Levite, the true tabernacle, and the true and final bloody sacrifice.

7. God determined the place of each tribe and its members and assigned their rank. This was an act of grace that gave them a part in His holy nation. Likewise, through Baptism, every Christian has been made a member of Christ's body, the Church, and has received His Spirit as a gift according to His will (1 Corinthians 12:11) for the common good (12:7).

God has made us partakers of Christ and, through Him, of one another in one body. That one body, with its one Lord, Spirit, and Father (12:4–6), as well as its one life, faith, hope, and Baptism (Ephesians 4:4–6), has its unity among many particular members. Whether we are made leaders like Judah or placed in positions of lesser visibility like Asher or Dan, we must recognize that God has created us all as one. His grace has not erred or cheated us out of His blessings. We do not need to covet the place or service of others or look down upon the "less honorable" members (1 Corinthians 12:21–26). Instead, we should always show respect and regard for them as members of Christ's body.

The role and service of individual Israelites was shaped by their place within the tribe and its life and responsibility in the larger community. The Law as God's Word, with its many statutes and commands, governed them. Under the Gospel, Christ has become our true tribe and the true Israel in whom we all share the same calling of faith in the Gospel and love to our neighbors. Though this unfolds in endless specific ways according to our individual lives, it is the rule of evangelical love that governs us (Romans 13:10; Galatians 5:14; 6:2; 1 Corinthians 12:30–31; James 2:8). Christians have been given God's love to empower, fill, and direct their lives, and this is the proper rule and sufficient grace to live God-pleasing lives (Galatians 5:22–23; Ephesians 5:2). By living in His redeeming love, we will be rightly guided to good works and unselfish consideration of our neighbor (Romans 13:8).

8. The types and shadows of the Old Testament serve as object lessons or pictures of the salvation that God promised He would bring about in His Son, Jesus Christ. Leaders (such as Adam, Abraham, Moses, Joshua), institutions (such as the Law, the Priesthood, the Crown and Davidic dynasty), and events (such as the Noahic flood, the exodus, David slaying Goliath), and other elements of the Old Testament foreshadow in imperfect ways the true and divine counterpart that God Himself would bring to pass.

As such, while their purpose is to show us Christ, the types themselves are limited. The tabernacle is a good example. Its physical dimensions limited access to it from only one direction, eastward. In order to enter the tabernacle, which only the Levites could do, it was necessary to be in the "right place." The tabernacle as a creation of the Law required adjustment to it and offered access only as one complied with its terms.

Christ as the fulfillment of the tabernacle provides entrance to men from all directions. The vision of the heavenly city in Revelation 21:1–13 reveals that three gates (perhaps also representing the Holy Trinity) stand open on each of the four sides. This is because Christ has opened the way for all men, since no one except He can conform their lives perfectly to the Law. The way He has opened up is the way of God's pure grace (Hebrews 10:19–22).

9. Jesus fulfills all three roles because He is prophet, priest, and king in one. God's Word calls for priestly service, which is what God's true king follows. Judah is the tribe from which the Messiah will descend (Genesis 49:10). While under the Law, these three works are parceled out among various men; they stand together as one in Jesus Christ. By hearing and believing Him, we follow the true prophet, the true priest, and the true king.

10. Reference to the death of Nadab and Abihu from Leviticus 10:1–2 is made in order to underscore the reality of human sinfulness and our plight under the Law. God's standard of righteousness is exacting, pure, and perfect, and not subject to compromise. Its demands are holy and must be strictly met. Failure to meet them meant the execution of justice, the punishment of the guilty.

While Nadab's and Abihu's actions themselves were sinful, by God's grace they nevertheless form a picture of Christ. He is the priest who offered Himself as a sacrifice and appeased the wrath of divine justice. Unlike Nadab and Abihu, Christ was innocent, the just dying for the unjust. And for that reason, because of His sinless sacrifice, the Law was fulfilled.

11. As mentioned previously, though not all Christians are public ministers, they are all servants and royal priests. Jesus Christ has sanctified our lives. In Baptism, we are made sharers of His life. By Him, our lives are freely and graciously made significant to God, full of divine purpose, and holy. Each and every moment is redeemed no matter how ordinary, all without our planning or purposing, because of what God has done for us in Christ. Zechariah 14:21 prophesies that under the Messiah (Christ) "every pot in Jerusalem and Judah will be holy to the LORD of hosts." This means that by Christ's sacrifice, not by any decision or action of our own, our lives are made vessels for God and all that we do in faith—no matter how secular, routine, or mundane— is before God a sacrifice pleasing to Him.

Lesson 2

God's Demands for Purity

Theme verse: *So shall they put my name upon the people of Israel, and I will bless them.*

Numbers 6:27

Objectives

By the power of the Holy Spirit working through God's Word, we will

- distinguish holiness according to the Law and the Gospel;
- value the service of the Office of Public Ministry;
- recognize what God's presence in Christ means for us;
- see Christ and learn how He is foreshadowed in Numbers.

12. In the Gospels, we read how Jesus cleansed the lepers by touching them. This was a stunning reversal of the way life had been under the Law. It had rightly demanded purity, but was able to do so only by excluding the unclean and separating the defiled from God.

In Christ, God reveals a new way: the Gospel. It fulfills the Law's holy demand for purity, but in a manner that reconciles people to God. This is because God in His mercy and through His divine power becomes one with them by assuming human nature as His own. He does so in order to take on all their sin on the cross.

We might say that under the Law sin's power is made stronger (1 Corinthians 15:56). When lepers are touched, defilement is communicated. In Christ, however, God's grace through the cross overcomes that defilement so that when lepers are touched, righteousness and purity that are transmitted to them.

13. The Law, once again, demands purity. This is good, right, and holy. God's ways are wise and life-giving. However, for sinners the Law's remedy for sin is always one that means guilt, judgment, and death. By it, sin is dealt with through exposing our guilt and shame and carrying out the sentence of justice.

We should not argue with the justice of the Law, since it is God's. Through the Law, our sinfulness and unclean condition are made manifest. However, because the Law results in the death of the sinner, it does not fulfill God's gracious will. For God desires not the death of sinners (Ezekiel 18:32; 33:11); He desires to bless humankind (Genesis 1:22).

So, in Christ, God deals with sin in a way that truly satisfies the Law and yet saves sinners from guilt, judgment, and death. By the cross, Jesus pays the due penalty for sin and fulfills the justice of the Law. Thereby He wins forgiveness for all people. In forgiving our sins for Christ's sake, God establishes in our lives real and lasting righteousness, which we receive through faith.

14. In Matthew 2:23, God's Word tells us that Jesus' being from Nazareth was a fulfillment of what was "spoken by the prophets." This prophecy is said to have been, "He shall be called a Nazarene."

Commentators vary on exactly how to understand this statement. Since there is no prophecy in the Old Testament put in exactly these terms, some have suggested it refers to an oral tradition ("spoken by the prophets") known in that time.

Others suggest that this is a play on words and harkens back to the Nazirite character mentioned first in Numbers and especially in the most famous of Nazirites, Samson. This is probably the best construction since it roots the passage in Christ Himself and not in unverifiable theories.

In any event, Jesus is the true Nazirite who devoted Himself fully to God. He drank only from God's Spirit and not the spirit of this world. His thoughts and wisdom were "uncut"; that is, they were not shaped by human judgments. He remained the resurrection and the life even though touched by death. In Him, we are counted alive, pure, and wise. We are called to live by faith and grow in His grace.

15. Numbers 6 and its purity laws remind us of how unclean we are and deserving of nothing but God's wrath and judgment. We fail to measure up and at every turn find ourselves as violators of God's Word and polluted with sin.

It is precisely at such moments, when the Law has done its dreadful work of smiting and slaying us, that we are ready for and stand in desperate need of God's grace. This is when God's Word of mercy and unconditional love may be seen for what it is and perform its glorious work of saving us and blessing our lives.

Only when we have been so troubled and brought to despair will we hear the Gospel and believe. God smashes our cruel idols of self-righteousness that demand so very much. God does this in order that we might know, believe, and worship the true and living God who freely gives us all things.

16. As we discussed previously, though all of our lives as royal priests are reckoned as a service to God that is pleasing to Him (we mean, of course, the life lived by faith and through the Spirit), the New Testament mentions certain things in particular as "sacrifices." These are *not* atoning gifts that pay for sins, though. Christ has accomplished that for us fully, finally, and forever. Rather, these offerings are what directly result from our lives as they have been given and have received God's grace. Knowing we are redeemed and that God in Christ vindicates us in spite of our weakness, sinfulness, and disadvantage, we offer the sacrifice of praise and thanksgiving. We confess and call upon His name in faith.

However, out of love, we also freely and generously make material sacrifices, but not for God's benefit. We do this to the benefit of our neighbor, those in need, and to Christ's Church.

17. The Levites were God's gift to His people. Through them, God's service of mercy and blessing was carried out in God's name and for their benefit.

In the same way, the Office of Holy Ministry (the Pastoral Office) has been instituted by Christ to bring to the world the gifts of salvation won for us by Christ (Matthew 10:8).

Pastors should be regarded as Christ's representatives. "The one who hears you hears Me, and the one who rejects you rejects Me, and the one who rejects Me rejects Him who sent Me" (Luke 10:16). They should be received as Christ's very angels (Galatians 4:14; Revelation 2–3).

18. The Passover was the first and greatest festival of the Jewish religious calendar. It commemorated God's deliverance of the children of Israel from slavery in Egypt as the fulfillment of His promise to Abraham (Genesis 15:13–14). Jesus fulfills the Passover because He delivered sinful humanity from its slavery to sin, death, and the devil. Holy Communion feeds us this very salvation. To neglect the Lord's Supper is to neglect Christ Himself and despise the gift of salvation. Such action is effectively one of self-exclusion. If impenitently persistent, it is valid grounds for the congregation to excommunicate such a member.

19. The tabernacle was always and ultimately meant to deliver a Gospel message. Its form was certainly that of Law. The tabernacle had a distinct legal character to it, with all the rules and regulations that had to be carried out by the children of Israel.

The tabernacle's final significance, however, was that it stood as a visible promise of what God Himself would do and bring about for sinful people. Sin had separated humanity from God and, as a consequence, Adam and his children had lost communion with Him. God, however, immediately shows His love and mercy and makes a gracious promise to restore humanity to fellowship with Himself (Genesis 3:15). He will erect a dwelling place where man and God will be one. This is ultimately fulfilled in the God-man, Jesus Christ.

The tabernacle reiterates God's promise and foreshadows in type how and what this will mean. The tabernacle is a picture of Jesus Christ Himself, God's true tabernacle, which is built by God and not humankind. We are made part of this building by being joined to Jesus Christ (Ephesians 2:22; 1 Peter 2:4–5). For this reason, the "building" of the Church and God's "work" must be recognized by us to consist properly of the pure preaching of the Gospel and the right administration of the Sacraments. The greatest service laypeople can render to the Church is to faithfully hear and gratefully receive the Gospel as public ministers share it to them. Whatever else they may do is a service to a neighbor that manifests God's love. Only as we are joined to Christ by the means of grace and through faith partake of His salvation are we involved in Christ's work and the building of His Church.

20. The visible action of the cloud and the audible sound of the trumpet point to God's Word. This reflects the generous and condescending mercy of God shown us in the sacramental forms of the Gospel. In Baptism and the Lord's Supper, earthly elements are joined to or taken up by God's Word of promise. In these means of grace we have a certain and concrete time and place in our visible, natural human world where God blesses us richly according to His Word.

Lesson 3

The Journey from Sinai to Kadesh

Theme verse: *My servant Moses . . . is faithful in all my house. With him I speak mouth to mouth, clearly, and not in riddles, and he beholds the form of the* LORD.

Numbers 12:7–8

Objectives

By the power of the Holy Spirit working through God's Word, we will

- grow in the patience of faith to endure with trust life's trials;
- learn to submit humbly to God's justice;
- deepen our reverence for God-appointed ministers;
- see Christ and learn how He is foreshadowed in Numbers.

21. Faith is created by the Word of God, the Gospel, working in our lives by the power of the Holy Spirit. Faith lays hold of the truth of God made known to us by that Word. This faith grows through exposure to the Word and Sacraments as we experience life in this world. The world's difficulties and disappointments are the seedbed, as it were, but not the source of our growth in faith.

The world and the flesh, as the natural ways of human life and understanding, are contrary to faith and the Spirit. They do not lead men into the way of God but only away from Him. The world and the flesh do not live by God's grace, power, and provision but by their own unholy resources. They proceed on the basis of their judgments of human reason and sense perception. This is because, of course, they have fallen under the power of sin.

Trials, then, are when we need God's promised grace because of some conflict, problem, burden, lack, and the like. God uses trials to cause us to look to His promise alone as the assurance of His grace. We trust that whatever the situation, God has acted in Christ to redeem us and is acting now on that basis to apply Christ's saving grace infallibly and lovingly.

22. The repetition of the marching orders is noticeable because it comprises a large portion of Scripture. It is not enough to refer to the instructions given previously. God repeats the orders given before and even adds a few new details.

This repetition is not at all unlike the recapitulation of the Law given in Deuteronomy. In fact, it is consistent with the repetition of other sections of the Law in Numbers from both Exodus and Leviticus. This serves to show sinful people's need for the Law; its repetition is needed. We lack righteousness and are convicted by our sin. Our lives are not in the right order, either in relation to God or others. By sinful human will or deed, we are incapable of being in the right place, at the right time, and in the right way, as it pleases God. God's Law reveals the perfect standard showing us that we are in disarray. Only by His Son's blood are we placed in the right order before Him. Only through Christ are we proceeding in life rightly related to God and others.

23. Numbers 10:35–36: "And whenever the ark set out, Moses said, 'Arise, O LORD, and let Your enemies be scattered, and let those who hate You flee before You.' And when it rested, he said, 'Return, O LORD, to the ten thousand thousands of Israel.'"

Moses' invocation of God was similar to other occasions in which God was called upon. It was an acknowledgement of His gracious presence, which came about for them by God's initiative and work. Moses did not invoke God's name in an attempt to bring God to the people. This is the practice of pagans. Their gods are far away and must be called upon with pleas for them to come to their fearful worshipers. Instead, Moses speaks God's name because He has promised His gracious benedictory presence.

However, this particular invocation and what was being called for from God was unique. His presence was invoked in connection with the ark's (and the people's) setting out and settling down. In both cases, a formal and distinct action takes place. The ark's movement or stationing defines that action. The ark was the place above which God's presence dwelt. Therefore, in both of these cases, God was acting for His people. He moved or settled in the process of leading them to the Promised Land. There Israel would face enemies that were, in fact, God's enemies. In this way, God's people were taught to find their entire life in Him.

24. Human reason determines that this judgment is excessive and somewhat arbitrary. However, we should not be surprised since God's judgments always seem wrong and unjust to sinful human wisdom.

Even if they seem contrary to our own human sense of justice, God's ways are perfect; it is our own ways that are actually perverse. This is hard to learn and really is not understood until God shocks us with a few practical examples. We are not offended, for example, when the Law prescribes a 20 percent recompense for theft. This seems reasonable enough. We take offense, however, when we learn what constitutes theft in God's sight and discover that *all* of us are guilty as sinners for taking what is not rightfully ours (this world and its goods).

However, God is merciful, and we are not consumed (Lamentations 3:22). The question we should be asking is not, "Why did God kill these people?" but "Why didn't He kill all of them?" By the Law, they and we all deserve death. Jesus put this question to people in His day (Luke 13) in regard to a famous disaster. A tower in Siloam had unexpectedly fallen and killed many people. The "good" died with "the bad," some thought. Others concluded that they must have all been "sinners" and that those who were spared were "righteous." Jesus knew the people were missing the point. He told them that unless *they* repented they would all perish in the same way—by God's wrath poured out in judgment.

25. The Church is God's people. They are called by the Spirit through the Gospel into communion with Jesus Christ. This communion comes about and is sustained by the means of grace through faith. Without faith, we prove ourselves false. God's Church is to be the community of faith in this world. By its trust in God's Word, the Church testifies to people about God's faithfulness and grace.

Because the Church's visible and outward life in this world is one in which false Christians will be found, it is essential for them to be aware of the ways in which such people will affect and attempt to influence churches. This will be manifest primarily in unbelief.

26. In John 6:22–58, the "rabble" would be those who just previously saw Christ's miracle of the feeding of the five thousand with two small fish and five barley loaves (John 6:1–13). They sought Jesus later in the same location and, not finding Him, looked elsewhere. They did this not because they saw a sign or understood the spiritual message or significance of the miracle, but because they thought He could be a perpetual source of natural food (John 6:26).

What they failed to understand is that Jesus' action was a display and provision of God's grace. Christ blessed the tiny portion of fish and bread and thereby made it the right, adequate, and needed food for those people. Their real need was salvation, God's free gift that is received through faith alone. In giving the people of Himself, Jesus taught them that by having Him added to all things, their emptiness was truly filled up and their life preserved in God.

Likewise, the manna on which the people of Israel lived was meant to show them that God is the giver and sustainer of life. Food without God is as good as starvation and death. Yet, even the slightest of meals, with God's blessing, is an immeasurable abundance. Faith apprehends God's sufficiency not in the outward form of our lives but in the promise of Christ's saving work placed in it for us. Thus, while what life "feeds" us may itself cause leanness and even death, we eat it in the utmost confidence because it is Christ on whom we truly feed through faith in all our lives.

27. God appointed these leaders to work with Moses under his supervision. They expressed God's good will to the people and His desire to show them His grace. God can just as easily accomplish His work without these men since He Himself is sufficient for the task whether using one man or many. However, He does this in order for Moses to know and believe His grace.

God condescended to Moses' limitations and showed that His power and grace can make such an accommodation and work under such circumstances and still achieve their saving ends. In one way, this is a picture of the humility of Christ.

As partakers of Moses and his spirit, these men are fit for service. Likewise, as we partake of Christ through faith by the means of grace, we share in all His grace (see John 1:16) and thereby are enabled to serve others according to the will of God.

28. The seventy-two (or seventy according to some manuscripts) are the New Testament counterpart to the seventy elders appointed under Moses. Here God's pattern of redemption reveals itself, teaching us that God's grace and blessing come to us through human hands appointed by Him for their bestowal.

The primary and crucial difference, though, is that while in Numbers this is indeed God's Spirit, it is His Spirit as mediated under the Law and by Moses. These elders carry out the ministry of the Law, judging the people. The Apostles and the larger band of ministers chosen by Christ share in God's Spirit as mediated by Christ. In Him,

God's Law is fulfilled and righteousness (or justice) is administered not through judgment but through the forgiveness of sins. Only in this way is God's true righteousness realized, one that leads to life and not death.

29. As with Miriam and Aaron, we often rebel against God by attacking those whom He chooses and by whom His grace works to bring us His salvation. We imagine that we are not being insubordinate to God because we convince ourselves that the faults we find are legitimate and proof enough that the public minister does not deserve our respect and submission.

However, it is really God we are despising because we believe that God would not use such a person, and we judge that no God worthy of faith and respect would do so.

God calls us to see Himself in these sin-scarred and blemished servants, though. This is because it is a reflection of God Himself, who is our servant and faithful minister only by taking on our form and bearing in Himself all our sins on the cross. This is good news because it means our salvation. We, who by the Law do not deserve God's blessing but only His wrath, are made holy unto Him and the objects of His benedictory grace through the cross.

30. Moses' intercession for the people is a recurring scene in the drama of Numbers. Time and again he must ask God to stay His hand of wrath and to deliver His people.

Miriam's sinful rejection of the divinely appointed authority of Moses placed her under God's wrath, even through she was Moses' sister. Aaron appealed to Moses to intercede. This is curious since Aaron as high priest was properly the one to approach God for mercy, but he could not. This shows the limit of his priesthood and the need for one that will transcend all bounds.

The ministries of Moses and Aaron are fully realized in Christ. In His name and by His unending intercession, we are delivered from ever being under the wrath of God (see Romans 8:34; Hebrews 7:25). Christ does this because He became a curse for us on the cross, and by His suffering and death for all our sins changed our standing before God in every way.

Lesson 4

Unbelief and Korah's Rebellion

Theme verse: *How long will this people despise me? And how long will they not believe in me, in spite of all the signs that I have done among them?*

Numbers 14:11

Objectives

By the power of the Holy Spirit working through God's Word, we will

- be warned about the peril and sin of unbelief;
- realize our need for Christ's intercession;
- repent of our natural tendency of rebellion;
- see Christ and learn how He is foreshadowed in Numbers.

31. Israel easily could be faulted for many things. Doubtlessly their daily routine was marked by lapses of various kinds. They suffered from all the imperfections for which a holy God could fault them: bad tempers, impatience with one another, foul language, disrespect to parents, and the like. In a mass of people numbered in the millions, sin was not lacking.

However, the sin of *unbelief* was the reason God punished them and denied their entrance into the Promised Land. Unbelief is the rejection of the grace of God that provides forgiveness. Unbelief rejects God's gift and, thereby, deprives the unbeliever of God's blessing.

The land is God's gift (Numbers 20:24) granted to them by His hand. Israel received the land as an inheritance given them by a promise (Exodus 15:17; Deuteronomy 4:21). Therefore, they obtain this gift through faith, trusting God to do what He has promised. Ten of the spies believed that God's power was inferior to that of the various inhabitants of the land and all their military might. They reckoned that there were forces God could not overcome. In the same way, when we disbelieve God's promise of grace, we judge Him unfaithful and unable to do as He promised and, thus, do not revere Him as the God of all salvation.

32. The land is said to be a place of rest (Deuteronomy 3:20; 12:9–10). It is the place appointed by God for their permanent earthly settlement with God in their midst. Here, they are no longer strangers and pilgrims but at home as citizens of the nation and possessors of the land.

However, Psalm 95 clearly shows that the promise of the land was not the ultimate significance of their faith. Even while in the land, they are exhorted to continue to hear God's Word of promise for rest and not to harden their hearts as did a previous generation. If the land had been all there was to the promise, nothing more would have been said.

This is what the writer of Hebrews says in chapters 3 and 4. There, we are told that if entrance into the land under Joshua had been the fulfillment of what the promise ultimately signified, then "God would not have spoken of another day later on" (Hebrews 4:8). The writer concludes that because of this there "remains a Sabbath rest for the people of God" (Hebrews 4:9).

This rest is portrayed to us as salvation, ceasing from our own works and entering into God's (that is, His work accomplished fully in Christ, Hebrews 4:10). Christ crucified is God's promise and the true object of faith. We are called by the Gospel to trust in His merits, His suffering and death. By these, He won for us the Promised Land of God's kingdom, and by these all our enemies—sin, death, hell, and the devil—have been overcome.

33. Upon hearing the unbelief of the people (spread to them from the ten other spies) and their pathetic bemoaning their plight, Joshua and Caleb tore their clothes in an open act of repentance (Numbers 14:6).

By doing this, they declared the action of the people to be sin and publicly marked themselves as standing in opposition to them. This was a consequence of their faith. They stood fast by God's promise and urged the people to believe that conquest was possible despite the humanly insurmountable forces that stood in their way. They saw God's promises and power *for* them as being greater than the threats and strength of the enemy *against* them.

This is the true fear of God: to believe that God's gracious power in Christ to save us is greater than sin's power to damn us. In the Christian Church, this is in many ways undermined by teaching and preaching that do not declare Christ alone the full and exclusive means of salvation. It also happens as churches judge the possibilities of God's grace on the basis of human will and resources. A church is planted, and its ministry directed not by God's promise but by a human plan that prescribes the nature and shape of ministry based upon secular models. People are made confident in themselves and not in God. Without these things, it is said, the church cannot and will not grow. Such words are the embodiment of unbelief.

34. At the heart of Moses' plea for mercy was his appeal to the Lord's name and the word of promise given in connection with it. God's reputation or "fame" (v. 15), as He who brought Israel into covenant, is at stake. His faithfulness and ability to perform what He swore will be brought into question.

Moses cannot mitigate the seriousness of this people's sin, nor can he ask God to suspend justice (v. 18). In a way that shows God's abundant mercy and upholds His Law, Moses asks for pardon.

This, of course, anticipates the mercy that God will bring to pass in Jesus Christ. In Him, God satisfies the Law and punishes sin to the fullest while providing an abundance of mercy that rescues sinners from all the guilt and punishment rightly due them.

God therefore shows mercy, but hides it in judgment. The nation is required to die before entering the Promised Land (with the exception of the remnant of faith in the two men Joshua and Caleb). However, from them He raises up another generation, who, as that seed made new, is able to enter the land. This, too, is a picture of Christ. He is the one in whom we die and are made new, and by whose death and resurrection we are made heirs and possessors of God's promise of eternal life.

35. The people have been warned not to attempt war against the Amelekites and Canaanites in the hill country. Their unbelief has brought down upon them the sad punishment of being denied entrance into the Land of Promise. God's gracious Word of promise was rejected, along with the faith it would freely bestow.

Now, by the force of will, they wish to prove themselves believers and violently make use of God's Word according to their own desires. They clearly believe that it is up to them to make the invasion happen and to rectify the situation by their actions.

This is little more than unbelief and rebellion against the Lord. Now they have disregarded God's counsel and rejected His Word again. It is certain they would insist their motives were sincere and that they meant to do right. They likely appealed to God's Word and offered other rationalizations. However, this effort was, as it was before, rooted in unbelief and therefore in every respect displeasing to God.

God alone is the object of our faith. God revealed in Christ is not only He who promises salvation, but also He who accomplishes it for us by His own power, will, and wisdom.

36. God speaks of the time when the people will be in the Promised Land. This places before them a promise fulfilled and reminds them that with God their end is known and already accomplished. This is what the people should have trusted in all along. Instead, their eyes and ears were diverted from God's Word, and they lost faith. Rather than beholding God's promise and looking at their lives in the light of His power, they looked to themselves and judged their condition and future by what they saw with human wisdom and natural sight.

However, now with the severe punishment of a generation being denied entrance into the land and dying under God's stroke in the wilderness, it seemed impossible for anyone to make it.

In Jesus Christ, God has already accomplished our justification. Even though we remain outwardly sinful and appear to the world anything but holy, the truth is that for Christ's sake we have been declared righteous in God's sight. The pilgrimage of the Christian life is one of faith that looks to God's mercy in Christ, and the assurance of His blessing, aid, and grace at all times.

Because of God's work for us, we can endure life as it is in this world until Christ returns. Outwardly, we share in all the miseries of this life, suffering the judgments of God common to all humanity because of sin. We do this because hidden in all of our suffering is God's grace. In Christ, God has redeemed us so that no matter what we suffer or endure in this world, we have God's kind and gracious Word of justification. In Christ, God tells us He is not against us but always and only for us (Romans 8:31).

37. Sin is serious and the judgment it brings is real and awful. Once again, Israel must learn this lesson from God. In order to show them what righteousness by the Law means, God sentenced a Sabbath-breaker to be stoned.

Curiously, we are told that he was kept "in custody" (15:34) until it was determined what would be done with him. The Law had previously instructed such criminals to be stoned (Exodus 31:15). It would seem here that Israel either doubted this or was following a careful procedure that ensured that only the Lord judged in capital cases.

Either way, the verdict of guilt called for a sentence of death. The Sabbath, the day made for humankind's blessing, was fulfilled under the Law through the curse of capital punishment. However, God did not make such a Sabbath for man. The Sabbath was originally created to be a blessing (Genesis 2:3), but sin ruined this creation gift by placing humankind under a curse. For all people, even the ordinary acts of life become sin.

This is why under Christ alone, as He fulfills the Sabbath, can it once again become a "delight" (Isaiah 58:13). Only through justification in Christ are our lives reckoned by God as meeting up to His Law. Living under His righteousness and the forgiveness of sins, we are set free from living for ourselves. Through Christ's merits, God sees Christ's holy will and good work in all our lives (our sins and their guilt being imputed to Christ on the cross).

38. Korah is like any person who lives in opposition to God-ordained authority, but especially false prophets and teachers. Unfortunately, all too often they are deceived by the devil. Like Korah, they are convinced by a distortion of God's Word that they do not have to show respect to the Office of Public Ministry or, ultimately, submit to God's Word. God had indeed made the whole nation "holy" by His presence (Exodus 29:43). However, this did not mean that all were called to lead and perform the work of Aaron or Moses.

In the New Testament, a man named Diotrephes resisted the apostolic and ministerial authority of John. Diotrephes loved being first, that is, in control (3 John 9). Such people fail to realize that the humble form of leadership in the Church that takes place through the Pastoral Office is designed to show Christ and allow for the exercise of God's saving power in our lives. They do not understand that divine shepherding takes place through human weakness and is shaped by the cross. The worldly wisdom and carnal ways of Korah despise God's ways and the cross (see Matthew 16:23).

Korah should have known better, being instructed by God's external Word, which is the means by which God's will is known and graciously done among us. However, such people follow their own whim, believing themselves more spiritual than those who follow the Word alone. They are filled with the ambition they mistake for zeal and lay claim to visions and impulses of "the Spirit" that are nothing but lusts for power and glory. God's people are sheep to be led, not cattle to be driven. Only the divine hand of grace, operating through the Gospel as it is ministered to us by rightly called and ordained men, feeds God's lambs in the way He desires.

39. Moses, as a figure of Jesus to come, stands between the living and the dead. Moses' mediation prevents death from swallowing up the living altogether. He stands between life and death for the sake of his people.

We must remember that in all of Moses' acts of intercession, he is not prevailing upon God to do what God is reluctant to do. Rather, Moses acts to show us God's will hidden from us by the Law, God's will in the Gospel. The Law is God's will known in one way, that is, as Law. For sinners, this will always mean guilt, wrath, judgment, and death. There is nothing else for sinners from God by the Law.

Yet, God wishes to save and bless, not damn and curse. So, Moses is moved to show and call for a mercy that cannot be seen in the Law. It is something that so far as the Law is concerned seems impossible. Something must change. God allows Himself to be "overcome," as it were, by Moses, who anticipates what God Himself will do in Jesus Christ. In Christ, God will become a man and die for sins in order to silence the Law and end its reign of terror and death over sinners.

Lesson 5

Aaron and the Means of Grace

Theme verse: *I have taken your brothers the Levites . . . They are a gift to you.*

Numbers 18:6

Objectives

By the power of the Holy Spirit working through God's Word, we will

- discover the divine gift that the Office of Public Ministry is;
- confirm our faith in the means of grace;
- be motivated by love to support the ministry of the Gospel;
- see Christ and learn how He is foreshadowed in Numbers.

40. Tempting God is strictly forbidden (Deuteronomy 6:16; Matthew 4:7; Luke 4:12). Tempting God means putting Him to the test, seeing what He will do. Doing so is an act of distrust and unbelief and an implicit charge that God's Word and character are suspect.

What of Malachi 3:10? "Bring the full tithes into the storehouse, that there may be food in my house. And thereby put me to the test, says the LORD of hosts, if I will not open the windows of heaven for you and pour down for you a blessing until there is no more need." Here, two things must be kept in mind. First, it is Christ alone who ultimately fulfills this promise. This is Law of the tithe. We can never *strictly speaking,* satisfy its demands. Second, this passage concerns what is given for the support of the Levitical service (see Numbers 18). Here, God promises that as they bring their tithes (in full) and all the commanded offerings, the grace of God the Levites are called to minister to them will be available in abundance. What God is calling for is faith to believe His promise of grace, not a childish exercise of "give and let's see what God will do." Faith already knows what God will do and is enabled to give by God's promise of grace that goes before. This is why plans to increase offerings by daring people to "test" God are unfit for Christian use (e.g., so-called "faith promise" schemes). They are little more than an appeal to human pride.

41. God has already identified Aaron as His chosen high priest. By His Word given to the people through Moses, Aaron was named high priest (see Exodus 28:1). Aaron's name is vested with divine authority and power by that Word, and for this reason alone it should have been evident which rod, or staff, would blossom.

The Christian Church is called to stand upon God's Word. She has the mind of Christ by which she knows and judges all things (1 Corinthians 2:15–16). When she lives by empirical proof, gauging and assessing matters as they appear before men's eyes and according to human reason, she loses her divine wisdom. The Gospel is the mark of the Church—the Word purely preached and the Sacraments rightly administered. By this alone, we know where Christ is present and which Church is truly His. However, when we judge by size, numbers, and visible and earthly glory, we are deceived.

42. In 1 Timothy 3:16, we are told that Christ was "manifested in the flesh, vindicated by the Spirit." This refers to the two stages of Christ's life, His humiliation and His exaltation. He revealed God to us by becoming flesh and living among us in our lowly state of weakness and misery. His life overflowed with justifying and forgiving mercy for sinners, and through Him the powers of the devil were overthrown. Yet, He was allowed to suffer and be seen as being no different than others, even dying upon a cross between two thieves. Those who heard and received His witness in faith, though, knew that He was the Son of God, since by Him God's Word revealed this to be so.

In the resurrection, our Lord blossomed with life like the rod of Aaron. God accepted His sacrifice, and His life proved itself innocent and righteous before God. Jesus gained His vindication not for Himself, since He was already personally righteous, but for us sinners, for the humanity whose nature He assumed to redeem.

43. Jesus is the true Aaron or high priest who sanctifies us forever by His service (see Hebrews 10:10, 14). He has performed all the work of our salvation, taking our sins to Himself (1 Peter 2:24) and bringing us near to God through His sacrifice (Ephesians 2:13; Hebrews 10:19). Thus, there is nothing left for us to do. What remains is for us to receive and live in this gift through faith alone. Our communion with God is established, secured, and maintained by Christ's work for us so that we may approach God without fear of wrath for our sin.

44. On the one hand, the tabernacle reminds us of our sin and God's holy wrath against it. The stern warning of judgment for any unclean person coming near it is a sure sentence of death. How could this possibly be avoided? Daily life in a camp of millions presented endless chances of defilement and with the tabernacle at the center of the camp, the threat of judgment was always near.

Yet, the tabernacle and the priesthood existed to remedy this very situation. They provided atonement that took away sin. With this in mind, the tabernacle assumed a Gospel character. One begins to see in the tabernacle the promise of salvation and God's gracious intent for sinners. However, this is not realized until sinners reckon with its legal character, its work as Law. Sin must be exposed and the need for God's mercy recognized.

45. Ultimately, it is God in Christ who takes responsibility for sin. Aaron stood in the place of God and bore the "iniquity connected with the sanctuary." This means that the guilt of the people, their unholiness, was transferred to Aaron and, thus, to God Himself. God does this as an act of mercy because it is only He who is truly holy and only He who can bear unholiness and live and remain holy. By bearing our sins and shame, God enables us to go free and live in peace before Him.

Christians do the same thing. By the power of the cross and that same forgiveness given to them in Jesus, they bear the guilt and shame of others. They are willing to be the peacemakers by returning good for evil, blessing for cursing, and love for hate. They forgive others and extend God's forgiveness in Christ to the whole world in this way.

46. "One who is taught in the word must share all good things with the one who teaches" (Galatians 6:6). Support for the Office of Holy Ministry remains the duty of love for all Christians. Gifts offered in the Church should be first and foremost to provide just compensation to called and ordained ministers of the Gospel and other church workers, as well (see Deuteronomy 25:4; 1 Corinthians 9:9; 1 Timothy 5:18). These gifts are enabled by divine love (2 Corinthians 9:7). If God's love in Christ fills our heart, it moves us to acts of generosity and appreciation (1 John 3:17).

All believers are seen in the Levites, as well. We are those whose inheritance and portion are not in this world but in God (Hebrews 10:34).

47. God has no need of anything, and neither does Christ. He reigns at the Father's right hand, and with the Holy Spirit as one God,

now and forever. However, He does receive and make use of the material gifts and possessions we offer in His name. We can never give enough, if that is what we strive to do. Jesus said when we have done everything commanded we are still only "unworthy servants" (Luke 17:10).

Therefore, God sets us free from the Law by paying our debt. We are poor, miserable sinners, worthless servants, on whom He freely spends His riches to redeem. His service sanctifies our lives and makes them holy vessels through which that same love is to be extended to others. Because of God's rich grace, we should be especially generous to those brothers of His sent in His name to minister that grace to us. By sheer mercy, He gave up His wealth to sustain us when we were covered with sin and performed His work throughout a world that was offensive to Him. Likewise, in that same mercy, we should support the ministers of the Gospel, though they are marred by the same defects, faults, and weaknesses with which we suffer. God has received and enriched us in Christ, and we should do the same, especially since they are dependent upon congregations for their earthly needs.

48. The rare, red heifer is an unusual animal that is provided only by a special work in nature. In an even more special work, Christ was conceived by the Holy Spirit in the womb of a virgin. The heifer is a female bovine, not a male bull. Christ assumed a state of humility and weakness and not one of external glory. The heifer was to be red, the color of blood and sin. Christ is the sacrifice that makes holy because He is the one on whom the sins of the world were laid. However, this heifer is not sacrificed in the usual way stipulated by the Law, but outside the camp on another altar. Christ was slain outside the gate, so that as the red heifer provided cleansing from all defilement, He might do the same truly and forever (Hebrews 13:12).

Finally, notice that the ashes—the victim's sacrificed body and blood, along with cedar wood (the cross), hyssop (the device for sprinkling), and scarlet yarn (redemption) all burned—are joined with water. Everything necessary for cleaning, the whole Law fulfilled, as it were, is put into water. Its use means the application of all those things to the unclean. In the same way, Baptism unites us to Christ, in whom the whole Law and all righteousness have been accomplished. His work is applied to us, and we received it through faith alone, and it suffices for the forgiveness of all sins and eternal purity before God.

49. Moses teaches us that no one is above God's Word and that all people are bound to the means of grace. God's power works

through earthly instruments that are, by design, lacking in the kinds of human power and glory that men consider necessary to accomplish great things. God joins His Word to feeble human words (Scripture, preaching, absolution) and ordinary and plain earthly elements (the water of Baptism and the bread and wine of Holy Communion). Through them, He applies the work of salvation accomplished by Jesus. Sinners are made new creatures; they die and rise again with Christ, the very Spirit of the Father and of the Son is given them as the insignia of their royal status and as the promise of eternal life. Satan and all the powers of darkness are overthrown and cast out, and the court of heaven declares them righteous!

The human eye, of course, does not see those things, but they nevertheless take place. God uses means that cannot possibly, by human considerations, do such things. He does so to nurture faith in Him and to preserve His glory. Faith alone apprehends His work and receives in meekness God's Word as wholly adequate and full of what it speaks.

Though the Lawgiver of Israel ("faithful in all my house," Numbers 12:7), Moses is a sinner and no different from those who fell in the wilderness. He is not righteous any more than those who died in unbelief. Yet, he teaches us that God alone is righteous and that only through faith in God's grace are we.

50. In the first instance, Moses was told to strike the rock (Exodus 17:6). Similarly, Christ was struck by God's wrath, the rod of judgment, in order that we might be given the water of life (see John 19:34). Since Christ fulfilled the Law, it is by the mercy of the Gospel that water continues to be supplied for us. Yes, we deserve judgment, but Christ bore God's wrath for us.

Lesson 6

Death and Destruction

Theme verse: *And the* L*ORD obeyed the voice of Israel and gave over the Canaanites . . . to destruction.*

Numbers 21:3

Objectives

By the power of the Holy Spirit working through God's Word, we will

- gain insight into the mystery of God's providence;
- see ourselves in the light of God's mercy;
- learn to stand boldly and not compromise the faith;
- see Christ and learn how He is foreshadowed in Numbers.

51. The Edomites are the descendants of Esau, Isaac's firstborn son and the brother of Jacob (Genesis 25:25, 30; 36:1, 8). Because of this, Israel took a nonhostile approach in their relations with them. An ancient pact between these two peoples was struck between the patronymic heads of each people (Genesis 33:4–16). Esau and Jacob (Israel) were reconciled and vowed to live in peace.

Israel honored this agreement, but Esau's descendants did not. Nevertheless, despite the lack of reciprocity, Israel acted peacefully toward them.

In the same way, Christ's mercy continues to overshadow this world and will do so until He returns. For now, it remains the day of salvation in which God's mercy is extended to all people, making the sun to rise and rains to fall on the just and the unjust.

A day of judgment waits, though. The prophet Amos foretells this as he charges Edom with breach of this covenant (Amos 1:9, 11).

52. Perhaps, the people were angry or disappointed. We know that delay is not denial. However, in the Christian life we must come to learn that, because it is God's plan that is always at work; *denial is not delay either*. Yet, by nature we react to such situations, deem them unwanted, and judge them to be unwise. We fret and quarrel with God

because we cannot see how this or that possibly serves our good or His glory.

Couldn't God just dispatch with the Edomites in one swift act of judgment? Why must He and we suffer the triumph and gloating of enemies? How does this show power?

Faith knows and sees that true victory means enduring and submitting to opposition and accomplishing one's ends through the very plans and devices plied in opposition. When these are taken up and made the instruments through which God's plans are realized, we are shown a power that makes us "more than conquerors" (Romans 8:37) and are given a faith that "overcomes the world" (1 John 5:4).

53. Moses presented Israel as those who, in the name of God and His mercies, were to be given consideration. The plea was not to any national glory, military prowess, or cultural prestige, but simply to the fact that they are poor slaves set free by God's mercy. There is nothing naturally in them that the Edomites would find appealing or compelling. In this respect, the Israelites are an image of Christ, who had "no form or majesty that we should look at him [that is, give Him special regard], and no beauty that we should desire Him [that is, desire the spiritual gifts of salvation and kingdom He came to bring]," but was instead "despised and rejected by men" (Isaiah 53:2–3).

Christians live the same way in this world. God's treasure is hidden in "jars of clay" (2 Corinthians 4:7). Our beauty is spiritual and hidden from the eyes of flesh, though revealed to the world like a city set on a hill (Matthew 5:14). We are outwardly weak and wasting away (2 Corinthians 4:16), bearing in our body the form of Christ's lowliness and death (2 Corinthians 4:10). However, God's Spirit renews us and marks us as God's elect (1 Peter 4:14).

54. Moses represents the Law and Aaron the priesthood of the Law. The Law's inability to bring about true and divine righteousness is seen in Moses' and Aaron's failure to fulfill the will of God. In the end, because these men are sinners, only unrighteousness and judgment are possible.

Their deaths are pictures of the limits of the Law. In Romans 8:1–3, we are told that righteousness, the true fulfilling of the Law, could only be brought about by God Himself. This He did in Christ by assuming sinless, human nature, and by taking to Himself our sin on the cross.

Jesus brings in a new and living way (Hebrews 10:20). The Law can only end in death. Yet, since Christ became flesh and took that death and the judgment of the Law to Himself, He has ended its reign and inaugurated the reign of His grace through the Gospel.

55. In the transfer of the priestly garments we see a type of continuing priesthood of Christ. The type has its limits as seen by the fact that the form of ministry under the Law could not sustain a priest forever. Each new priest meant the previous one was obsolete (Hebrews 7:12, 23).

Christ, on the other hand, receives an eternal priesthood, according to the order of Melchizedek (Hebrews 5:6, 10; 6:20; 7:11, 17). In His exaltation, our Lord continues the priesthood carried out on earth so that in *one person* the type is fulfilled. Christ is both Aaron who dies (and with him the former administration) and Eleazar who, by Aaron's death, receives the priestly vestments in exaltation (on top of Mount Hor). Thus, it is said that Christ "by the power of an indestructible life" (Hebrews 7:16) and by a continual life and permanent priesthood is able to "save to the uttermost [that is, in every way, fully, finally, and forever] those who draw near to God through Him, since He always lives to make intercession for them" (Hebrews 7:16–25).

In all the forms of worship, we see this set before our eyes. The Lord's Supper shows us that the living Christ and the crucified Christ are one and the same as He feeds us the very body and blood given up in death on the cross.

56. Many of our churches still retain crucifixes both on their altars and the walls of their sanctuaries (or the nave proper). This is in no way a denial of the resurrection, as some claim. Rather, it is the appropriate form for visibly portraying and remembering Christ's sacrifice among us just as the Babe in the Christmas crè che reminds us of His birth. Our lives are lived under the sign of the cross with glory hidden beneath our crucified, mortal frames. Joy is hidden in sorrow, righteousness under sin, and life in death. We are penitent worshipers whose joy is of the Spirit and not the flesh, whose exaltation is the sublime reality of God's mercy poured out upon us as we humble ourselves in contrition. God's true witnesses are clothed in sackcloth (Revelation 11:3). This is not because there is any doubt or lack of certainty about God's grace and forgiveness, but because this is how we are to be found before God in a sinful world. Christ crucified is life to us and the path of faith under the cross. Though outwardly marked by sin and suffering, this path is stocked with life, grace, and joy because of Jesus.

57. Our Lord calls us to deny ourselves (to judge as sinful and, therefore, useless all the ways, judgments, and powers natural to us) and take up the cross (receive God's grace in Christ that makes good all our lives) and follow Him (Luke 9:23). Christians can rightly and faithfully testify to Christ only in this way, that is, as martyrs. They dare not attempt to "sell" Christ or make Him or the Gospel pleasing to the diminished appetites of this world. They are not to seek or expect the favor of the world (John 15:18–19) or judge their lives or the ministries of their congregations by popularity or the numbers of people receiving the Gospel (1 Corinthians 4:5).

The Church on earth is in a militant posture and must be ready to expect the Gospel to bring spiritual conflict (Matthew 10:34). We must count Christ's Gospel, not our lives, as precious; therefore, we are to maintain a pure confession no matter how great our earthly loss (Revelation 12:11) or how few side with Christ (1 Peter 3:20; Revelation 3:4).

58. The word *Hormah* means "destruction." It becomes a memorial designation that recalls for the Israelites God's thorough judgment. Contrast this with God's judgment among the people back in chapter 11 and how the place of His chastisement was called "Taberah," or "burning." The difference between them is that, on the one hand, God deals with His enemies by destroying them, while on the other hand He deals with His people by purifying them.

59. Aaron's death reminds them of how grave the sin of unbelief can be. This holiest of people failed to enter the land because of it. This is a lesson for all of us to believe God's Word and cast away all doubt.

Lesson 7

Look and Live

Theme verse: *And if a serpent bit anyone, he would look at the bronze serpent and live.*

Numbers 21:9

Objectives

By the power of the Holy Spirit working through God's Word, we will

- learn more of the extent of the Gospel's saving work;
- discover the power of faith;
- gain appreciation of the grace of God;
- see Christ and learn how He is foreshadowed in Numbers.

60. Our impatience, like that of the Israelites, is due to the paucity of faith. We believe God hates us or is out to get us, and, therefore, each visible obstacle is an indication that He doesn't care or is leaving us high and dry.

The truth is that while God has every right by the Law to pour out His wrath upon us and leave us to the miseries and frustrations that come with sin, He loves us and is working to bring us to faith at every turn. He makes Israel endure a test to cause them to see their sinfulness and His grace (Deuteronomy 8:2, 5).

Because God has brought an end to the reign of sin and death in Jesus Christ, we can endure knowing that all our lives are blessed by His grace and sanctified as instruments through which He works in us to believe in Him and partake of His blessings and life (Hebrews 12:10).

61. Perhaps without realizing it, we consider the Gospel worthless. Yet, the Christian Church and the lives of Christians are created, made to grow, and are fruitful only by the Gospel. Therefore, what is the Gospel? It is the forgiveness of sins.

The old Adam despises the Gospel as weak and powerless. His is the way of Law. He believes that by force of command, human willing and doing, through goal-setting, and pressure tactics of the flesh and worldly motivational techniques he can extort good works from God's children and cause Christ's Church to grow.

The Gospel does not satisfy the carnal spiritual appetite of the old Adam, but, in fact, denies him such and makes him weak and lean. However, it feeds the new man life and grace until full. The Gospel seems like "nothing" to the world and the flesh, since it calls for only faith. There are no great works and grand accomplishments except Christ crucified. Feeding on this, though, makes one a partaker of that work, the work of God (John 6:29).

62. By lifting up a bronze serpent, the people are forced to see their sin transferred to another. They are also called to look away from themselves and trust that by seeing their sin on another, or rather the judgment of that sin, that their deadly wounds are healed (see Isaiah 53:5). They are not to examine themselves and look at the place of their bite and judge for themselves that this is so. By faith, they must fix their gaze on the bronze serpent raised up before them.

In Christ, God—raised above us and on the cross—takes to Himself our sin. By His becoming defiled with sin we are made clean, the just for the unjust. This is God's supreme revelation of Himself to His people. Although He could have shown them His power in one way by forcing the Edomites to allow them passage, God had something better planned. Through their "sin" He brings them salvation and shows them a power in grace that overcomes in a way that does not destroy others but saves them.

63. As stated previously, this world is full of sin and death. However, in order to redeem it, God sent His eternally begotten Son into the world to assume human nature to pay the penalty for sin by His death on the cross. God cast His lot in with us that we might have our lot cast in with Him.

God turned the tables on sin and death. The cross is the saving instrument by which this takes place. We see that in the most unjust act ever perpetrated, God brought about the greatest righteousness; through the most wicked of intentions, His good will came to pass; in the darkest moment of human history, the light of God shined brightest.

This is how it *must* be, though, since God's ways and man's ways are utterly opposite (Isaiah 55:8–9). All human righteousness is unrighteousness to God, human wisdom pure folly, human power vanity, and human glory is shame in His sight. Therefore, God takes up what people in their proud wisdom and self-righteousness consider worthless and makes use of them as His holy means. In this way, God brings us to faith in Himself and enables us to bear witness of His truth, righteousness, and grace by enduring every evil of this world. We bear up under all these things—even death itself—because in them God has placed His crucified Son who has conquered them by His cross.

64. Faith saves not because of any virtue or power in itself but because of its object. Faith is filled with that to which it looks in trust and clings in hope. Faith is, therefore, credited with all the virtues, powers, and glory of its object: Jesus Christ. When asked by His disciples what works they should do in order to carry out God's work (how presumptuous and arrogant of sinful humans to think they can do *God's* work), Jesus replied, "This is the work of God, that you believe in Him whom He has sent" (John 6:29).

Faith grasps and takes to itself the work that God Himself performs for sinners, the saving work of Christ. As it receives with trust this work performed on its behalf, faith is made one with it and obtains all its accomplishments.

65. Paul declared that God "in Christ always leads us in triumphal procession" (2 Corinthians 2:14). This is not the result of our decisions, thoughts, actions, or motives. Such a boast of triumph is made solely because Christ has redeemed our sinful lives. Only faith can make such a claim because of the merits of Christ. Nothing else will justify our sinful lives. Since Jesus by His suffering and death redeemed us, He has won us back from the power of sin and the devil. In Baptism, He joined us to Himself so that now our lives are defined and determined by His good will, work, and purpose. We are called to live by faith trusting that this is so for our salvation and God's glory.

66. The wells of salvation (Isaiah 12:3) were dug out for us by the divinely royal hands of the Son of God. In fact, Christ as the Son of God is the proper heir of all things (Hebrews 1:2). God's kingdom is for Him (Psalm 2:6–8). However, He ever so kindly wishes to make us sharers with Him in it. So out of pure mercy and sheer grace, He works in the "earth" and digs deep enough to obtain the water of salvation. God's gracious provision of this water typifies the salvation He will bring to pass (and has) through His Son, Jesus Christ.

67. All songs—especially canticles—that extol God's mercy and confess His salvation in Christ do the same as this short verse in Numbers 21:17–18. In the preaching of the Gospel and the

administration of the Sacraments, this is done as well. When a pastor absolves our sins and comforts our afflicted and terrified consciences, this is done. In every way, the Divine Service centers around and observes what God has done in Christ, His condescension for our deliverance from sin and death. By His humiliation, His sweat, blood, and toil, Christ dug the well of salvation for us. All we are called to do is drink these gracious and life-giving waters and give voice to the praise and thanksgiving that they cause to overflow from our lives.

68. Faith is the posture and perspective of the Christian life. This means looking at and living in light of the truth revealed and the salvation accomplished by Jesus Christ. The native ways of the old Adam are under judgment, and its powers and judgments have no place in our lives spiritually. Christ crucified is our wisdom and power, which defies the natural ways of human life (due to sin).

69. The command not to fear is one of Gospel. This is not issued as a Law that must be fulfilled but as a reality of life to be believed. Faith is made possible by God's saving grace in our lives. "Do not fear" graciously affects the hearer, thereby demonstrating its Gospel character.

Lesson 8

Balak, Balaam, and Baal

Theme verse: *You shall not curse the people, for they are blessed.*

Numbers 22:12

Objectives

By the power of the Holy Spirit working through God's Word, we will

- become aware of how God's grace protects us;
- understand what God's blessing means in our lives;
- recognize how Satan works to undermine our faith;
- see Christ and learn how He is foreshadowed in Numbers.

70. The New Testament warns of both the "error" (Jude 1:11) and "teaching" of Balaam (Revelation 2:14). These are summed up as the "way" of Balaam, referring to his practice of ministering for gain (2 Peter 2:15).

Balaam is a false prophet whose motives are personal increase (whether of money, material possessions, influence, or power) and self-glory. He seeks praise, reward, and recognition for his religious work. This is evident in that King Balak knows he can be bought and sends "the fees for divination" (22:7, 17).

Christian churches are guilty of this when they measure their life and ministry by material and financial gain, considering it "success" and good stewardship if their bank accounts and holdings increase and failure if they give more than they receive. In fact, the measure of our lives is not how much we gain but how much we lose in the selfless life of love that gives away all to others (Luke 12:13; 16:1–15). This may not make for a favorable accounting of things among people, before committees and others, perhaps, but it will bring from God, the true and final judge of all, the happy words, "well done, good and faithful servant" (Matthew 25:21).

71. King Balak had certainly heard of Moses. The reference to the Exodus of the people, "a people has come out of Egypt," means that

reports of this stunning and unprecedented event had reached his ears. However, he clearly knew Moses was unapproachable and his services not for sale.

Also, Moses' fate is bound up with his people. Unlike Balaam, Moses pays a price to be the prophet of God's people. His only gain is *their* benefit (see 2 Corinthians 12:15). In fact, when they curse him and accuse him time and again of being a false prophet, he responds with blessing and prayers of intercession for their salvation.

Lastly, Moses leads God's people to faith in the Gospel and the true worship of God that the Gospel brings. Balaam is always working with his hidden agenda of spiritual seduction to draw men away from the Gospel, justification through faith, to the dead works and idolatry of Baalism.

72. Despite the fact that Balaam was used by God to pronounce a blessing upon God's people, we are not to conclude, therefore, that God sanctioned his religion. Our Lord Jesus Christ is present everywhere, filling all things in heaven and earth (Ephesians 1:23; 4:10). He is present in synagogues, mosques, and every cultic temple. That presence is hidden, of course, and those worshipers do not either worship Him or worship rightly in any way. Nevertheless, He is Lord of that space and place, as well, and in ways hidden to the world (but revealed to be so in His Word and seen through faith alone) Christ is present working "all things according to the counsel of His will" (Ephesians 1:11).

This teaches us two things: first, that we may be confident that Christ in His lordship has mastery over all things (sin, death, hell, and the devil) for our good and His glory; second, only where His presence is graciously made known and the gifts of salvation communicated—where the Word is purely preached and the Sacraments rightly administered—may we gather to worship.

73. Balaam, as with so many false teachers, may compromise many of his principles. Not so with God's people. The reason is simply that all false religion at its heart is not truly *for* anything, but is in reality *opposition to* the truth. To be sure, deceived leaders and followers of false doctrine will tout some pet heresy and error as to what they are all about. Yet, since we know this is spawned by the devil, and people are drawn to this by lusts of their flesh that are set at enmity with God (Colossians 1:21), what is actually happening is a revolt against God (see Romans 1:18–32).

So long as Balaam can insinuate himself into the faith of Israel, he can smuggle in his corrupting doctrine and ways. He is perfectly content to worship in the name of Yahweh, so long as he can, inch by inch, influence, shape, and redirect the faith of God's people.

This is why no false teaching of any kind or to any degree must be permitted in the Christian Church. It is like leaven, or yeast, that slowly and almost without detection spreads until it permeates the lump of dough into which it was placed (1 Corinthians 5:6–8; Galatians 5:9).

74. Balaam's donkey is a poignant picture of the mercy of God for sinners given in Jesus Christ. Like this animal, Christ becomes a beast of burden who bears our load of sin. He is smitten and beaten for His good work of saving us from the sword of divine destruction. Likewise, He alone is the true and faithful witness who, in contrast to those who appear to be God's spokespersons but in truth are not, speaks only the Word of God.

Balaam is being taught that God's desire even for him, the false prophet, is that he be saved. God's mercies extend to him too. This lesson underscores why God will not have His people cursed, sinful though they be, but blessed.

75. By the Holy Spirit, Paul tells us that sinners were redeemed from the curse of the Law "by becoming a curse for us" (Galatians 3:13). As God's people, we stand under His blessing because through the cross our sin was removed by God Himself. In its place stands God's loving favor and salvation, His eternal benediction.

The cross disarmed the dark powers of this world (Colossians 2:15). Until our Lord's death and resurrection, death was a power that terrorized people. Hebrews 2:15 says that death was the devil's instrument of fear. Baptized into Christ, we share in His victory and live under His lordship at the Father's right hand, "with angels, authorities, and powers having been subjected to Him" (1 Peter 3:22).

76. The first two oracles seem to have reference to the present and describe the status of Israel before God at that time. They are a blessed and forgiven people. In other words, their sinful past does not define them, but God's grace does.

However, the latter two prophecies are oriented to the future, and the relation between the future and the present is significant. Their present status in God's grace is due to a promise to be fulfilled, the promise of a Redeemer-King who will accomplish in the earth God's righteousness. So, they are a people of God because of their future, and yet, this future is true of them now and even before this time (bound up with God's eternal purpose of salvation), since their past is swallowed up by this promise of grace.

Clearly, these words refer to Christ, God's true Jacob. The loveliness of His tent is the beauty of the righteous life He lived (and lives) tabernacled in human flesh (John 1:14). We share in that as we are hidden in Him by Baptism through faith (Colossians 2:11–12). We live in *His skin!* Christ is the King who, in His exaltation (Numbers 24:7), is lifted up above all persons and powers (1 Corinthians 15:27; Ephesians 1:2–22; Colossians 1:15–18; Hebrews 1:13).

77. Although we cannot say for sure, this ancient oracle was likely preserved among the non-Israelite nations. Balaam was a seer of the first order, and his words were highly regarded and received as sacred. Adding to this were the unusual circumstances surrounding this prophecy. The tradition of a "scepter" or king rising from Israel and its parallel description as a "star" rising from Jacob, could very well have been the source of speculation and study by astrologers for centuries. Think of the intrigue that continues over the false prophecies of the French prognosticator Nostradamus, though they are nearly five hundred years old.

78. Moses' absence is conspicuous. Since his failure at Meribah, his role has diminished. He will soon be replaced by Joshua, who will be named his successor even before Moses dies (Numbers 27:12–23). Moses is the great Lawgiver and stands for the administration of God's rule through it. His great sin reminds us of the impossibility of the Law to bring about true and divine righteousness when at work among sinful men (Romans 8:3).

God Himself must act, and, in meeting the opposition of Balaam head on and dealing with him directly, we are given a foretaste of the incarnation. Everlasting salvation and eternal righteousness come only when God Himself acts to bring it about (see Isaiah 25:9; 45:17; 51:8; 61:10; 63:5).

79. The New Testament applies the story of Balaam to us in a spiritual manner. In Revelation 2:14, 20, the false doctrine and worship that had crept into the churches of Pergamum and Thyatira are characterized in language that echoes in Numbers 25:2. We need not imagine that the idolatry was overt. In all likelihood, what was taking place was a spiritual compromise under the name of Jesus. A Christian form of things was retained (the "appearance of godliness," 2 Timothy 3:5), but its essence, the Gospel, had been lost.

This occurs today when we do not preach the Word of God purely, but mix it with or subject it to a test of human reason, science, our imaginations and feelings, or any other source or authority. This also occurs when we mix Law and Gospel. If these errors are committed, it results in God's children being fed false doctrine, not the pure manna given to us in Christ. It fosters reverence of an alien spirit, a spiritually adulterous heart, which practices infidelity to Christ.

This is why we are called to repent and believe the Gospel. Jesus Christ is our Lord and teacher, and His true pastors are called to feed God's people the pure and unmixed milk of His Word (1 Peter 2:2). Only then will Christ be worshiped and rightly so.

Lesson 9

The Second Census and Instructions

Theme verse: *Let the* L*ORD . . . appoint a man over the congregation who shall go out before them and come in before them, who shall lead them out and bring them in, that the congregation of the* L*ORD may not be as sheep that have no shepherd.*

Numbers 27:16–17

Objectives

By the power of the Holy Spirit working through God's Word, we will

- appreciate how God shepherds His people;
- remember what the true fear of God is;
- recognize the lavish generosity of God's saving grace;
- see Christ and learn how He is foreshadowed in Numbers.

80. Nearly seven hundred years before, God had promised Abraham that He would make him a great nation (Genesis 12:2–3) and multiply his descendants as the stars of heaven (Genesis 15:5; 22:17; 26:4; Exodus 32:13) and as the sand of the sea (Genesis 22:17). God did this despite all of the powers of sin and hell working against Him and them. God accomplished this for Abraham's descendants and did so by His own will and work.

This reminds us that God's promises are unilateral. This means that they are not dependent upon us, but are made with the promise that He by Himself will fulfill them (Galatians 3:16–20). God's people are the recipients of His saving grace and loving care. They are called to a life of faith that does not depend upon *both* themselves and God, but upon God alone to fulfill what He promised. Despite all our sin and weakness, our shortcomings and failings, He has pledged to "fulfill His purpose for me" (Psalm 138:8) and will bring to completion the good work He began in us (Philippians 1:6). "He who calls you is faithful; He will surely do it" (1 Thessalonians 5:24).

Sometimes it is said we should pray as if everything depended upon God and work as if everything depended upon us. This is nonsense and nothing but double-mindedness displeasing to the Lord. Only if and as we work depending wholly upon Him will our works be those that are acceptable in His sight, since they trust in His mercy in Christ to make them good.

81. Numbers 26:8–10 briefly recounts the fate of Korah and the 250 men who followed him in his attempted coup of Moses. These are men who did more than sin; they despised the grace of God and rejected its gift to them of Moses' leadership.

God is truly long-suffering and patient with us (Numbers 14:18). He provides atonement for our sins and desires that we believe and trust the sacrifice made on our behalf by Jesus to be truly sufficient for all righteousness. However, when we calculate to sin and exploit His grace for wicked ends, we risk losing it altogether and bring judgment upon ourselves. God has no wish for this, but by our own evil wills we destroy ourselves. We refuse His grace by rejecting the imperfect human hands of those ministers whom He has called to bring it to us.

82. By custom and ordinary law, daughters at this time had no claim to inheritance. Yet, God in His grace makes a way for what by standard legal practice was not permitted. The insistence of these women is an appeal to God's grace; it is an act of true faith. This is not unlike the Canaanite woman of Matthew 15:22–28. She had no standing with Christ by the Law; she was not a Jew. Nevertheless, she persisted in her faith because she saw (as it was revealed to her) God's grace in Christ. In this, she proved herself far more a child of Abraham than the self-righteous Jews who believed God owed them salvation.

This contrasts with Moses, who, of all people, could expect a place in the land of promise. And, yet, Lawgiver and holy man that he was (Numbers 12:7), it was not enough. His failure is contrasted with that of the daughters of Zelophehad to teach us again that righteousness comes to us by grace alone and through faith alone.

83. Joshua is a type of Christ whose service and leadership foreshadow the true shepherding that Christ will fulfill.

By His death and resurrection, Jesus has won for us freedom from all our enemies. We are released from the devil's power (Colossians 1:13) and the guilt and grip of sin (Romans 6:7). All things are ours (1 Corinthians 3:21) and made clean unto us by Christ's blood

(Luke 11:41). Every space is holy to us, ruled by His love and grace. In Christ, we are gathered back to God (1 Peter 2:25). None of this is done or is made so by any willing or working on our part, but is wholly God's work accomplished in Jesus Christ. He fulfills the Law because we cannot. If salvation were in any way dependent upon Joshua being Christ, it would never happen. Instead, salvation happened because Christ became the perfect Joshua.

84. Joshua is a portrait of grace and of Christ. Being neither Moses nor Aaron, he rightly should not have been able to enter the tent. He should have been struck down. However, we find him freely doing so as Moses' assistant. What does this mean?

John points us to the perfect righteousness of our Lord Jesus Christ. He was by nature righteous. Therefore, in all His actions, he did what was right and pleasing to God; that is, all His ways "followed" Moses (that is, the Law, or God's righteousness, John 8:29). At His Baptism, He was acknowledged by the Father to be His beloved Son. His life was lived by faith in the perfect liberty that was His as God's Son. Joshua, similarly, went into the tabernacle not presumptuously but as Moses' assistant, in accordance with his station. It was necessary since his whole life was devoted to being at Moses' side. His trust was in God that if this required him to enter the tabernacle, God would see to it that He would make the matter right by His grace.

Jesus Christ is that grace for sinners. He has entered into the highest heavens, God's very presence, for us (Hebrews 6:20; 9:12, 24). At His side, joined to Him in Baptism, we may approach God's presence unafraid and with confidence (Hebrews 10:22).

85. All of these appointed sacrifices show us the costliness of Christ's sacrifice and the divine wealth expended in His atonement. In the body that God prepared for Him (Psalm 40:6–8 and Hebrews 10:5–10), all that is prefigured in the sacrifice of both the animals and other substances, is fulfilled. God spares nothing, but gives over to death His treasures in order to ransom us from death.

We might miss this if we think of Jesus as a mere man dying on a cross outside Jerusalem. By looking at His sacrifice in light of Numbers 27–29, we realize what great spiritual riches were embodied in Him and poured out for our salvation. The value of His death is revealed to us. God holds nothing back, but empties the purses and pockets of heaven—His very heart—in order to deliver us from eternal death.

God's true desire is for a righteousness that the Law can only picture and outline. He desires all that the Law (fore)shadows to be realized in human flesh, in a life lived in accordance with His will. This is what Jesus did, and His righteousness remains for us to be bestowed upon us by the means of grace and to be received through faith alone. It really is finished! (See John 19:30.)

86. Hebrews 12:14 says that without holiness "no one will see the Lord." This holiness is a gift given to us freely in Jesus Christ (1 Corinthians 1:30). We are made partakers of Him through faith alone (Ephesians 3:17; 2 Timothy 3:15; 2 Peter 1:1–4). To grow this faith and strengthen our hold on eternal life (1 Timothy 6:12, 19), God sends afflictions by which the old Adam is weakened and the new man is allowed to grow (2 Corinthians 4:16). God forces us to flee to His mercy for refuge (Hebrews 6:18).

Through this we are hidden in Christ and are found in Him having no righteousness of our own but only that which comes through faith in Jesus (Philippians 3:9). God works to reveal the futility and wretchedness of all our self-righteousness. He employs the Law to make sin increase (Romans 7:9, 13), thereby causing us to see our need for His grace in Jesus Christ and trust in Him for righteousness through His blood (Romans 7:24–25). In this way, God prepares us for heaven.

87. The law of vows is a reflection of God's own faithfulness and immutability (His unchangeableness). Hebrews 6:18 notes that God vowed salvation to Abraham (and for the whole world) by swearing in His own name to do so. Thus, by His oath and in accordance with His own nature, He guaranteed salvation. We, on the other hand, are promise breakers. We cannot keep God's Law by our will or power. God alone brings to pass these promises (2 Corinthians 1:10).

Lesson 10

War and Settlement

Theme verse: *This land shall be your possession before the* L*ORD.*

Numbers 32:22

Objectives

By the power of the Holy Spirit working through God's Word, we will

- learn the value of pure doctrine and worship;
- recognize the true equity of God's grace;
- grow in our commitment to preserving the unity of the faith;
- see Christ and learn how He is foreshadowed in Numbers.

88. The infamy of Israel's sin at Peor (chapter 25) was especially offensive to God. We are reminded that, contrary to popular belief, not all sins are equally bad and heinous. Certainly, all sins damn, but they do not all involve the same degree of moral or spiritual turpitude. The Scriptures distinguish between sins of weakness and ignorance and those of a deliberate and willful nature (Numbers 15:30–31; 1 Timothy 1:13).

The corruption of doctrine and worship is just such a sin. It is blasphemy and a direct violation of the Second Commandment. The deceitful attempt by the Midianites to pollute the faith of God's people through the false counsel of Balaam and turn them to idolatry and sexual immorality aroused God's holy anger. This was more than the persecution of His people, though that was bad enough. It was an assault on the Lord Himself and a scheme to rob God's people of the Gospel. Drawing them away from faith in God's grace and His free promise of righteousness to a worship that sought by dead and sinful works to gain these was apostasy. His people were severely chastised, but His enemies were destroyed in the fury of His vengeance.

We should learn from this account that God's will is for us to keep the faith once delivered to us (Jude 1:5). We cannot suffer the Lord's name to be invoked where other gods are called upon, no matter what the circumstances. We must resist the seduction of the "prince's daughter" (Cozbi, Numbers 25:15, 18), that is, the Jezebel spirit of this world that always tempts us to compromise (Revelation 2:20).

89. In our Baptism, we were joined with Christ, dying and rising with Him. Through this gracious work of God, the powers, wisdom, and ways of our flesh and this world were put to death. God's judgment was carried out on them (Galatians 6:14).

We are called to live in our Baptism, seeing that our earthly passions have been crucified (Galatians 5:24) and that we have risen with Christ to a new life of faith in God's grace (Romans 6:4; 7:6). Putting off the old (Adam, the flesh) and putting on the new (Christ, the Spirit) means believing God's promise and work of Baptism has really taken place and is true of us. The Spirit now fills our hearts with holy desires and affections through faith by means of the Gospel (Colossians 3:12). It is the impulse of love that now guides our steps.

90. Sexual sins, fornication in particular, have powerful and lasting effects in human life. Sex is a sacred gift to people, meant to consummate the marital union of a man and a woman as husband and wife. It mystically and physically weds body and soul and is designed only for marriage (Hebrews 13:4). It has been vested with deep natural powers that affect the human psyche and body at every level.

When this area of life is opened up to sinful abuse and demonic spiritual forces, a joining takes place that is hardly different from possession. The whorish spirit of the devil grips our lives and plunges us into a life of unspeakable shame and moral degeneracy.

The moral degradation of Canaanite worship and the sexual perversion it sponsored had radically infected the people of those nations. Their cultures were nothing less than demonic, inhabited, and tyrannized by demons. God would not risk His people being infected with these evil forces and, therefore, orders the complete destruction of the Canaanite societies. Not a vestige of their existence was to remain.

91. In Jesus Christ, God has made us coheirs with His Son (Romans 8:16–17). All the riches of heaven have been made available to each of God's children. The plunder and spoils of His salvation are shared equally with every Christian. In Revelation 21:7, the promise is made to those who conquer through faith in Jesus Christ that they will be partakers of Christ's heritage. The sonship that He has by nature He will grant to them by grace.

Although Christ is the true warrior who alone engaged in the agonizing battle against the devil and won, we are made to partake in

His victory through faith. Consider John 1:16, "And from his fullness we have all received, grace upon grace." The phrase *grace upon grace* could be translated "grace answering for grace," meaning that every gift and blessing that exists in Christ is ours. Its presence in our lives corresponds to its existence in Jesus.

Repeatedly, Scripture tells us that Christ has revealed and communicated to us "all things" that are His from the Father (John 15:15). It is the Spirit's ministry in our lives to show us these good things through the Gospel and, by making them known, to cause us to possess them through faith. These are righteousness, faith, love, God's power, the intimate and blessed knowledge of God, the Holy Spirit, joy, peace, and many other heavenly gifts.

This is what God desires to see in our lives. The tribute He is owed is nothing but His own image and name that have been restored to us in His Son. The Gospel grants us these in Christ and, by faith alone, they dwell in our hearts (see Matthew 22:20–21).

These gifts are distributed to us by the means of grace. God has established the Pastoral Office to steward these means and minister them to God's people so that His gifts might be given them.

92. In the Midianite war, Israel seemed blameless. God ordered this act of judgment (Numbers 31:2). The victory was total. God's providence and favor prevented the loss of even one Israelite soldier. They were unscathed.

Still, Israel is not without sin. Why? Because even in all our holy works, prompted by God, we still sin. As Paul said by the Holy Spirit, "So I find it to be a law that when I want to do right, evil lies close at hand. . . . Who will deliver me from this body of death? Thanks be to God through Jesus Christ our Lord! So then, I myself serve the law of God with my mind [or spirit, meaning his life of faith], but with my flesh I serve the law of sin" (Romans 7:21, 24–25).

The officers knew, as did Paul, that their sinlessness was owed to God's grace. He has made atonement possible. While under the Law, these officers must provide the gold; under the Gospel, God provides it for us. These men are a picture of the Gospel, showing that God Himself in Christ will furnish the gold of heaven to make atonement for us.

So, daily we live by the "gold" offered up on our behalf, that is, the blood of Jesus (1 Peter 1:18). This cleanses us from sin and all unrighteousness (1 John 1:7–9).

93. Sadly, in the history of the Christian Church as it is visibly known, too often there is a record of its becoming enamored of this world and its riches. It covets worldly power and esteem. It has imagined that acceptance and acclaim by the world will validate Christ and the Gospel. It measures itself by its size and influence.

Our hearts and affections should be set on the promise of the world to come (Luke 18:30; Hebrews 6:5; 10:34) and the riches poured out upon us from Christ, at God's right hand (Colossians 3:1). When this one hope given to us by God from Christ is common to all, the Church experiences the unity of faith and the Spirit. Human interests and carnal ambition are set aside, and God's people are united by the Gospel. Their hopes and aspirations are directed by the spiritual graces of the Gospel, and they are, thereby, enabled to live at peace with one another in this world.

However, when worldly dreams and a lust for earthly glory and power govern the Church's life and ministry, discord ensues. This is often masked under pious talk of evangelism or church programs, but, in fact, it is demonic deception (James 3:15).

94. This concession to Reuben and Gad is one of grace. This is land outside the Law; it is not, legally speaking, holy territory. However, God by His grace makes it so, even placing six Levitical cities on either side of the Jordan (Numbers 35:14). Similarly, our sinful lives are not holy territory. They are out of bounds, alien land. God, however, by His grace in Jesus Christ, takes this to Himself and makes our lives and land His own. Through the cross, our lives are redeemed, sanctified, and marked as God's dwelling place (1 Corinthians 3:16; 2 Corinthians 6:16; Revelation 21:3).

Lesson 11

Review and Regulations

Theme verse: *And you shall take possession of the land and settle in it, for I have given the land to you to possess it.*

Numbers 33:53

Objectives

By the power of the Holy Spirit working through God's Word, we will

- value the lessons of the past;
- witness how God's mercy is the story of our lives;
- observe God's pastoral care of our lives;
- see Christ and learn how He is foreshadowed in Numbers.

95. The stories of the Old Testament are given for our edification, both as Law (1 Corinthians 10:1–14), warning us of God's wrath for sin, and as Gospel (Romans 15:4), encouraging us with God's promise of grace to endure through faith.

As we look back at our lives, we can see many high and low points. The path winds circuitously. It looks to us like anything but a straight and level path. Yet, that is precisely how God sees it and what He has made it to be for us in Jesus Christ (Luke 3:5). He is the one who, by His righteousness, vindicates and makes good a record that would otherwise be crooked and full of blemishes and sins.

96. The way things are before the face of people and the way they are before the face of God are as opposite as day and night. God's way of righteousness is completely opposite and different from humankind's. Therefore, when He accounts for life, it will reveal a record unlike what human judgment and analysis would expect.

Those who live by faith in the righteousness accomplished and provided by Christ for sinners appear in God's sight to be blameless and holy in all their deeds (1 Corinthians 1:8; Ephesians 1:4). So complete is God's forgiveness of our lives that we will not come into judgment (John 5:24). By this is meant a judgment of condemnation.

Rather, because we have Christ's righteousness, the final judgment will be a public vindication of our sinful lives (Proverbs 4:18).

This record of Israel's wandering in the desert excludes mention of their sin because it is an account made by the Gospel and not the Law. Through it, they are absolved of all their sins, and God's own saving purpose and righteousness are seen.

97. See question and answer number 90. The seven nations dwelling in Canaan were thoroughly polluted by sin. The stain of moral corruption touched every facet of their cultures. They were dominated by satanic influence and filled with evil spirits. Before God, they were an abomination and had to be totally eradicated.

Human reason finds this offensive. It raises ethical objections based upon claims of the innocence of people and a lack of love by God. However, sinners are in no position to question the justice of God. In Job 40:2, God asks, "Shall a faultfinder contend with the Almighty? He who argues with God, let him answer it."

The fact is, people have been sold into sin. God has every right to punish all people with death. No one is innocent and without sin in His sight (Psalm 14:3; Romans 3:10, 12). Beyond this, though, we must remember that God has redeemed humanity through His Son, Jesus Christ. Therefore, the punishment of death inflicted upon these people is not the final word. Jesus Christ has joined all people in death in order to rescue them from death.

Strangely, this is precisely the work God performs in our lives through Baptism. Consider how in 1 Peter 3:18–21 Baptism is said to be the fulfillment of the flood of Noah. In that act of God, death washed over the world as it was swept away in the waters of judgment. Noah emerges from the waters to a new world after the water subsides. Likewise, we are made to die with Christ in order that through death and judgment we might be raised to new life with God.

98. By seeing the land as God's gift, the people learn to treasure it as sacred. Their lives are sanctified because God has marked the boundaries of their lives as holy. They need not imagine that God has forgotten or neglected them. This land is where He has chosen to place them. His care and grace to them are thereby made evident.

Christ is the true heir of all things (Hebrews 1:2). The entire world has been made holy space by His redemption. Seeing our lives in light of this aids us in appreciating the sacredness of every moment and place we find ourselves. God has filled each experience of life with His sanctifying and benedictory grace. Knowing and believing this fills us with peace and confidence.

99. Contrary to what some ministers may teach, God by His own will and work has determined our salvation and inheritance. The tribal chiefs of Numbers 34:16–29 typify God's own wisdom and counsel by which He apportions to men His gifts.

In Matthew 20:21–23, we find the mother of James and John seeking from Jesus a way to secure high rank and honor for her sons in the world to come. She seeks gain for herself and her sons.

In stark contrast, Jesus' own mother gave up her Son. His purpose in this world was not to secure for Himself glory and honor, but to win salvation for others. This selfless consideration for the lives of others above His own was possible because He had received from the Father the promise of life (Psalm 16:10–11; Acts 2:31; 13:34–37).

Likewise, God's gracious counsel in Christ has given to us the promise of life and glory with Jesus (2 Timothy 1:1, 9). It is foolish to believe that by our works we will win what God has already obtained for us in Christ and has promised to us freely. The life of faith rests and trusts in this promise. By doing so, it can perform true good works and genuinely show the love of God to neighbor. Otherwise, life becomes a self-seeking endeavor and a pursuit of personal gain.

100. These little villages portray the pastoral life that God would have manifest in every congregation that bears His Son's name. They are a beautiful picture of life under the Gospel. Here, the pastures are large and the city small. The principal work is that of caring for sheep and allowing them to graze. Absent from this is the loud clamor of the market, the pressure of the boardroom, and the hectic pace of the city.

Our personal lives may be this way and, in this world, mostly are. Our bodies are made weary with the demands of life, but the soul should be at ease and made to rest in God's green pastures and soothed by His gentle streams. God wishes to do nothing but fatten up His precious lambs with the Gospel.

101. Christ is our place of refuge. In Him we are safe from the accusing voice of the Law. Even better, though, in Him we have found a permanent home. By adopting us into His family, Christ makes God and His kingdom our native land. There is no need for return since in Him we are united with God and made citizens of His realm. In fact, we are made heirs with the promise that we will rule with Him in glory forever (Revelation 22:5).

102. God's promise to us of an inheritance in heaven resolves any issues for us of what our future will be like. His grace has secured a life of heavenly bliss that will be endless. Revelation 21:4 says there will be no more sorrow, no pain, and that all tears will be wiped away. This means eternal satisfaction.

This makes possible a life of contentment. Our lot is God's and His is ours. We come to learn how to be satisfied with His blessing (Philippians 4:11; Hebrews 13:5). In this way, the Lord truly becomes our portion (Psalm 16:5; 119:57; 142:5).